Rich Student. Poor Student.

Your Guide to Growing Wealth While Studying

Peter J. Middlebrook

ISBN: 979-8-9940805-0-4
Published By: Peter J. Middlebrook

Disclaimer
This book is an original, standalone work. It has no connection, endorsement, sponsorship, or association with the Rich Dad Poor Dad series, its authors, publishers, or affiliated entities. All ideas, methods, stories, and guidance presented in this book are solely my own and have been developed independently for students seeking practical approaches to building wealth while studying.

Rich Student. Poor Student.

'It feels like a father figure guiding you, giving you the kind of advice many people never had, practical, clear, and genuinely life-changing.'

Nova Hanson-Wilks
University of Wolverhampton Business and Law School

Peter J. Middlebrook

Why I Wrote This Book for You

I was the Head Boy in my school, the head of my rugby, athletic, football and fishing teams, but I left school without a single qualification and am now a self-made multi-millionaire. A paradox, if you like.

Most of you have been taught to believe that life only truly begins once you finish formal education. That's nonsense. Most people won't finish their undergraduate degree until their mid 20s, a graduate degree until their late 20s or early 30s, and a PhD not until their early 30s! That means the first two to three decades of your life put you at a huge economic disadvantage. If you want to become independently wealthy, your investment journey starts now, not once you conclude being a student.

While studying is a privilege, it still makes great sense to invest your student years in becoming investment savvy and financially literate, because building wealth takes time and requires a deep understanding of money, risk, and business. It also calls for an abundance mindset, so that you learn to see opportunities that other people miss. Schools rarely teach students about the value of investment, because most education systems are structured around academic disciplines rather than real-world investing and business practice. As a student, you are usually being trained to think like an employee and a consumer, not an owner or a producer.

Lessons learned at school are academic. Lessons learned in life are not. Practice makes theory, not the other way around. Yet the markets of the future demand skills not yet known, let alone taught.

I wrote this book because you don't need to wait for permission to start your life. School didn't work for me. Life did. And that's why you need to understand how to build personal wealth now; before the post-education traffic light turns green.

Peter J. Middlebrook, 2025

Rich Student. Poor Student.

CONTENTS

List of Figures

List of Tables

Abbreviations and Acronyms

AI	Artificial Intelligence
ASIN	Amazon Standard Identification Number
BLS	U.S. Bureau of Labor Statistics
BNI	Business Network International
BSc	Bachelor of Science
CBDC	Central Bank Digital Currency
CV	Curriculum Vitae
ETF / ETFs	Exchange-Traded Fund(s)
EU	European Union
FBA	Fulfilled by Amazon
FHA	Federal Housing Administration
FIRE	Financial Independence, Retire Early
FOMO	Fear Of Missing Out
GDP	Gross Domestic Product
GRE	Graduate Record Examination
HECS-HELP	Higher Education Contribution Scheme – Higher Education Loan Program
HCA	Hopkins Consulting Agency
IPO	Initial Public Offering
IRA	Individual Retirement Account
LLC	Limited Liability Company
MBA	Master of Business Administration
MVP	Minimum Viable Product
NFT / NFTs	Non-Fungible Token(s)
NGO	Non-Governmental Organization
OECD	Organization for Economic Co-operation and Development
P2P	Peer-to-Peer
PhD	Doctor of Philosophy
REIT / REITs	Real Estate Investment Trust(s)
SaaS	Software as a Service
SEO	Search Engine Optimization
STEM	Science, Technology, Engineering, Mathematics
UK	United Kingdom
US / U.S.	United States
VA	Virtual Assistant
VAT	Value Added Tax

Peter J. Middlebrook

FOREWORD

Ami Tadaa (Broccoli Mum)
Social Media Influencer and Businesswoman

Growing up, I was lucky to have a dad (Peter J. Middlebrook) who believed that education didn't end when you left the classroom. He showed me that the most valuable lessons are the ones you carry into your real life — how you think, how you act, and how you choose to build your future. His work ethic, resilience, and constant drive to improve himself shaped how I see the world. And in many ways, this book is the natural extension of the lessons he taught me from day one.

When I left university with a business management degree from York St John, I knew one thing for certain: I didn't want to spend my life working for someone else's dream. I wanted to grow my own ideas, solve problems, create value, and build something that mattered. That instinct — mixed with a lot of trial, error, and perseverance — led me to start my first company, the UK's first artisan vegan cheese business. It was niche, pioneering, and far from easy, but it taught me that students aren't limited to the paths they're traditionally shown.

A few years later, after losing 30 kilograms through eating a whole-food, plant-based diet, I created Broccoli Mum — a social media–based recipe and weight-loss brand that now generates over US$79,000 a month. But that success didn't appear overnight. It came from long days, uncertain steps, learning new skills, building habits, trusting myself, and showing up even on the days I doubted everything.

That's why this book matters. Students today face debt, pressure, and a world that can feel stacked against them. But with the right mindset, the right habits, and a willingness to think differently, they can build a life far beyond the one they're handed. This book gives students those tools; practical, honest, step-by-step guidance for getting ahead, staying out of debt, and building confidence in their own potential.

My dad has always inspired me to dream bigger, work harder, and create boldly.

I hope his book inspires you to do the same.

Ami Tadaa
2025

Rich Student. Poor Student.

MOTIVATION

I Hated Formal Education but Loved Learning

I am a self-made multi-millionaire and every lesson and strategy that I have learned might be instructive for you. You are just starting out, most of you rely financially on your parents or student loans. Instead of learning how the real world works, you are trapped in a cycle of essays and exams, competing with other students for grades that will not shape your future. The belief that scoring the highest grade guarantees real-world success is a myth. While education is the single greatest investment you can make in yourself, much of what you are taught will not prepare you for the world that will come knocking at your door the day after you graduate. Let us not forget, there are more unemployed or under-employed people with master's degrees and PhDs languishing on the job market than you can count on a million hands.

Many of you have been attracted into courses that are fascinating to study but almost useless when it comes to getting a job or building a family life. Think of ultra-niche degrees like medieval poetry, boutique peace and conflict programs that offer no practical skills, obscure philosophy subfields, or experimental art forms with no real market. Universities keep inventing ever narrower courses to fill seats, but the job market for these specialisms is tiny. You may love the subject, but if no one is hiring in that area, you're training yourself for unemployment, not for a viable career.

Peter J. Middlebrook

I am one of the few – perhaps the only – person in my family who has built inter-generational wealth. The many lessons I have learned can transform your life if you are willing to think differently. You face uncertainty, debt and ambition in equal measure, and you search for a life that feels meaningful rather than mechanical and managed.

I was never a natural academic. I was, by instinct, a maverick. I grew up in Worcester in the Midlands of the United Kingdom. I poured most of my energy into everything outside the classroom. I led through sport, music, and movement. I was the drummer in a rock band, watching people, rhythm, and life from the back seat.

I had brilliant relationships with certain teachers. The ones who could inspire. The ones who looked beyond the edges of their subject and saw students as people with potential. But many simply taught by rote, offering content that was dull, disconnected from real life, and nothing to do with the person I wanted to become. Like most students, I found those classes painfully boring.

After school, I worked on building sites while figuring out who I was and what I wanted to do. Eventually I left England at 18 years old and began traveling the world, hitchhiking from England to India, crossing up through China, taking the Trans-Siberian back into Europe, then hitchhiking through the Sahara Desert and onward into South America before finally returning home a much wiser man. I had a huge appetite for reading and devoured everything I could find along the way, learning about people, history, culture, conflict, and human nature in its rawest form. That journey was the beginning of my life. Life became my university. It was intense, unforgiving, exciting, and unforgettable. That was my real education.

In time, I went back and completed my undergraduate degree. I later earned a PhD part-time while working with the British Government and the European Union in Africa, advising presidents and prime ministers. I have since advised governments and businesses across more than fifty countries, own property on three continents, and built successful businesses that created real wealth in the real economy.

None of this came from lecture halls. It came from entering the arena where decisions matter, where markets demand results, and where second place is simply the first loser. The real world is a tough teacher, but it is also the most honest and rewarding.

This book is for students who feel they are being taught everything except what truly matters. Most education systems are designed to produce obedient employees. They do not teach the nature of money, how a business actually works, or how markets behave. They rarely teach how to spot opportunity, how to create value, or how to understand people. Most universities are full of academics who have never built anything of substance in the world beyond their campus.

You are told to complete your degree, get a job, pay your debt, and expect life to begin afterwards. Yet most graduates walk out with a certificate in one hand and confusion in the other. They leave with loans and no strategy for building a future. They are trained to follow the system, not to design it. You may know the phrase, 'I do not want to be a product of my environment, I want my environment to be a product of me', from the film 'The Departed'[1]. That became my way of life.

I wrote this book as both an entrepreneur and a father. My daughter is also a self-made millionaire. She did not wait. She began early, while she was still a student, and built momentum long before graduation. That is exactly what I want for you.

If time is money, then your student years are among the most valuable years you will ever have. You have energy, curiosity, flexibility, and access to people, ideas, and networks. This is not a waiting period before adulthood. This is your launchpad. Your springboard. The ignition point for everything you want to build.

This book is for students who refuse to waste years drifting, accumulating debt, and waiting to be told what they are allowed to do. It is for those who want to accelerate whilst everyone else is standing still. In short, I believe you do not have to wait until you graduate to establish your own business. You can lay the foundation for it now and use those three years productively to generate short-term wealth, but more importantly to build a foundation of knowledge and real-world

---

[1] Blake, W & Costigan, B 2006, *The Departed: screenplay*, Paramount Pictures, Los Angeles.

experience so that when you leave with your college degree, you are already operating in the marketplace as a successful entrepreneur.

I am fully aware that many people aspire for careers beyond the entrepreneurial world, including roles in government, international organizations, or research institutions. Those paths demand different skills and different temperaments, so not everyone needs to read this book. But for those who are destined for the private sector, the lessons here are critical for identifying who you are, choosing the opportunity that fits you, committing to it whilst still a student, and gaining the experiential learning of life at the same time as your academic education. In a world where much of what is taught at undergraduate level may leave people woefully unprepared for a real job, learning the skills, acumen, savvy, and understanding outlined in this book are perhaps the most critical lessons you will ever learn.

Inside these pages, you will learn how to see opportunity where others see nothing. You will learn to think differently, break lazy assumptions, and build things that matter. You will learn to understand people, recognize value, and position yourself as the person others trust to solve problems

This book isn't just a critique of the system; it's a toolkit for breaking out of it. Inside, you'll find real-world strategies, clear models, and practical tactics that show you how to earn, invest, build, and grow your own income while you study. Whether you want to freelance, start a business, or simply stop bleeding money every semester, what follows will show you exactly how to begin building your financial life now, not after graduation and not at some vague point in the future, but right now.

Wealth, at its simplest, comes from solving a problem, meeting a particular need or desire. Someone pays you for it. That is business. That is value creation.

This book cuts through the fluff, the jargon, and the academic fog and replaces them with tools that work in the real world. Practical. Clear. Action-focused.

Be bold. Be a maverick. Go right when everyone else goes left. Make noise when everyone else is silent. Where bold colors stand out, don't blend in. That is how you stand out. That is how you attract opportunity. That is how you win.

This is your time. Let us begin.

1. WHY YOU SHOULD READ THIS BOOK

A Shortcut to Building Personal Wealth

The universe is roughly 13.8 billion years old, and human beings have existed for only the tiniest flicker of that time. Your life – like mine – is a very small footnote in the vast enveloping cosmos – at best. While you may feel like you are going to live forever, the simple truth is that every second, hour, day, month and year of your passing will never return. Most students reading this book will already have spent most of their lives in education yet have not yet turned any of that learning into a single dollar. Why? This is because you have been conditioned to think education first and income second.

For example, if you complete a bachelor's degree in the United States, you will typically spend around 18 years in formal education (from kindergarten through to university graduation), with an average graduation age of around 24. Assuming you begin full-time work within the first year of graduating, and retire at 64, you will likely spend 40 years in the workforce unless you retire early. For most of you, the years spent in education would represent 45% of your total working life.

Furthermore, most of you will only begin to understand how to earn an income after you hit the job market because that is when you leave home and start paying your own bills. Most of you will be employees, or self-employed in the gig economy. A far fewer percentage of people become business owners and investors. Why is that? Well, formal education is largely taught by employees, not by the people who generate wealth. Sadly, financial literacy and investment have never been a formal part of national curricula, unless you study an MBA. You are – for the greatest part – taught to be an employee and a consumer.

Your Brain is Your Hardware – How You Think is Your Software

Everyone's born with a brain (obviously), but most never tap into more than a fraction of its full potential. I have always seen that your brain is the hardware, and how you think is your software. If school has hardwired employee and consumer software into the way you think, you will spend your life chasing jobs instead of making investments. To be self-employed, you need to run software built for speed, agility, and market awareness. Further up the food chain, a business owner needs to run software that sees opportunities where others see problems, but also that sees and manages systems, scale, and risk. As an investor you need to be running the software that thinks about returns, timing, and compounding. In other words, you can't be running employee software and expect investor outcomes. If you want different results, you need a different operating system, one that rewires how you think about value, money, and the world around you.

The problem? Most education systems train people to think like employees—designed by employees, delivered by employees. It's a loop that leaves millions unprepared for wealth creation. This book is here to break that loop. It won't turn you into a student millionaire overnight, but it will introduce you to the core principles of financial literacy, basic investing, and entrepreneurial thinking. The goal is to help you make the most of your years in education, not as time spent passively accumulating debt or sitting on the sidelines, but as a time to begin building real-world experience, developing income streams, and laying the foundations for future independence. Even modest steps taken now can prevent you from slipping backwards financially—and for many, they can be the beginning of meaningful progress.

What This Book Will Give You

Rich Student. Poor Student.

To position yourself for real life, you need more than good grades or a polished resume. You need the right mental software. That means understanding how the world works, how opportunity forms, how value is created, and how ideas turn into action. Whether you build alone or with others, you will need to rewire your thinking so you can spot leverage, navigate risk, and move decisively. The education system will not teach you any of this, so you will have to learn it on your own.

If you have ever felt the frustration of studying material that never seems useful, this book gives you a second leg to stand on. It turns your education into part of your life now rather than training for a distant future. Ivan Illich's *Deschooling Society* showed me that education systems are often built for control as much as for learning. Schooling shapes obedience more than creativity. Sir Ken Robinson highlighted that modern schooling came out of industrial revolutions, where students go in as a batch and come out as a batch, prepared for an industrial world. If your brain is your hardware and your thinking is your software, then being trained as an employee programs you to live a life designed for someone else.

It is no surprise that many of the wealthiest and most influential people were the so-called nerds at school. Many of them, like me, never flourished in the classroom because we were busy trying to understand ourselves. Our energy went into figuring out who we were rather than ticking every academic box. My daughter studied business administration, yet when she ran my investment magazine in the Middle East she realized that university had taught her nothing she needed. Her real learning came from doing. Time is precious. You can party and socialize as a student (that allows you to be with your peers, form networks, learning how to communicate and lead), but you also need to lay foundations that move your life forward.

While advising the President's office in Egypt, I visited a parent-run self-school where students chose each day whether to learn indoors or outdoors. It separated those suited to academic learning from those who thrived through experience. One young woman with Down syndrome had been classified as special needs in Germany. Within two years in the self-school, she mastered four languages. When she returned, the system did not know how to classify her. It proved that brilliance exists everywhere, and the wrong school can bury it.

To Be an Employee, Self-Employed or an Investor

Across the advanced economies of the West, such as the United States, the United Kingdom, Canada, Australia and much of the European Union, around 85 to 90 percent of people will spend their working lives as employees. A further 8 to 12 percent will be self-employed, often operating in the gig economy or running small solo enterprises, and only about 3 to 5 percent will become business owners who employ others. The pattern across major Asian economies is similar, though with greater variation. In countries like Japan, South Korea, China, India and those in Southeast Asia, roughly 70 to 85 percent of the workforce are employees, while 10 to 25 percent are self-employed, a figure that rises in emerging markets. As in the West, only a small minority, typically 2 to 5 percent, become business owners with employees.

Average Incomes for Different Job Categories

Employees in both Western and Asian economies typically earn the lowest average incomes because their earnings are tied to fixed wages, limited bargaining power and the number of hours they can personally work. If you don't figure out how to earn money while you are sleeping, you will only be paid when you are providing physical labor. Self-employed workers usually earn more than employees, but their income is volatile and highly dependent on personal effort and market demand. Business owners who employ others consistently earn far higher average incomes because they capture the value generated by a team rather than by their own labor alone. Investors sit at the top of the income ladder because their money works independently of their time, allowing them to earn returns even while they sleep.

In broad terms, income tends to follow a recognizable hierarchy across most economies, even though different economies have different average wage levels. Employees typically earn the least, as their income is fixed by wages and hours worked. If you are self-employed, you may earn more, but your income remains unstable because it depends directly on personal effort and the extent of available opportunities. Business owners generally earn more (though they also bear the full risk and cost of financing) again by leveraging systems and teams rather than their own time. I started as a day laborer and migrated to be an owner and investor. Investors sit at the top of this hierarchy because their income scales independently of their labor.

This logic closely mirrors the income structure popularized by Robert Kiyosaki in his *Cashflow Quadrant*, which distinguishes between employees, the self-employed, business owners, and investors as fundamentally different economic roles (Kiyosaki, 2000). These categories pre-existed Kiyosaki's work. This book builds on that framework, not to promote any ideology, but to help students understand how income mechanics operate in the real world and how early choices shape long-term outcomes.

The data broadly supports this pattern. In the US, median full-time employee earnings in 2025 are approximately US$ 62,000 per year (U.S. Bureau of Labor Statistics, 2025). Average self-employment income varies widely by sector but typically ranges between US$ 52,000 and US$ 68,000 (Federal Reserve Bank of St. Louis, 2025). Small business owners who employ others frequently earn over US$ 120,000 annually, reflecting the ability to capture value generated by a team rather than by individual labor alone (U.S. Bureau of Labor Statistics, 2025). Table 1 shows average incomes for different categories according to the US Bureau of Labor Statistics (2025).

Table 1.	USA AVERAGE INCOMES	
Category	**USA Typical Income Range**	**Notes**
Employees	About US$62,000 per year	Median full-time wage and salary earnings
Self-employed	US$52,000 to US$70,000 per year	Highly variable, depends on industry and workload
Business owners (with employees)	Often US$120,000+ per year	Earnings scale with the output of a team, not individual labor
Investors	No fixed average, often significantly higher than other groups	Income based on returns on capital, not hours worked

Source: U.S. Bureau of Labor Statistics (2025) *Usual Weekly Earnings of Wage and Salary Workers, Second Quarter 2025*

The Mounting Cost of Your Education

As universal access to education is no longer free—capitalism has eaten that right—most students graduating are significantly in debt.

The cost of higher education has risen sharply across advanced economies, leaving many graduates with substantial debt at the point they enter working life. In the United States, the average federal student loan balance for bachelor's degree borrowers stands at approximately US$ 39,075 (Education Data Initiative, 2025).

In England, students completing full-time undergraduate degrees in 2024 carried average student loan debts of around GBP 53,000 at the point of repayment, equivalent to roughly US$ 67,000 at prevailing exchange rates (House of Commons Library, 2025).

Canadian university graduates in the 2023–2024 academic year typically held student loan balances of approximately CAD 18,545, or around US$ 13,200 (Government of Canada, 2024).

In Australia, the average undergraduate HECS-HELP debt was approximately AUD 27,640, equivalent to around US$ 18,000, with repayment periods commonly extending close to ten years (Finder, 2025; ABC News, 2024).

Taken together, these figures illustrate a shared structural reality: students in many developed economies are entering adult life carrying historically high levels of education-related debt, often before they have built stable income, assets, or financial resilience.

Why Should You Read This Book?

Well, I wish that I had read a book like this when I was your age and if you're ready to stop waiting and start building, then this book will give you the tools to do exactly that. I have designed this to help you turn your student years into a springboard for improved income flows and streams, greater self-confidence, and real-world capability. Here's what you'll be able to do:

- Transform your student years into a period of income generation rather than debt accumulation.

Rich Student. Poor Student.

- Use your time in education as your most valuable resource and lay the foundation for your economic future long before graduation.

- Acquire practical money and market skills that traditional education rarely covers.

- Learn to think like an entrepreneur, business owner, and investor, not just as a future employee.

- Develop the mindset and way of thinking of a producer so you can identify and act on opportunities early.

- Build confidence by earning with limited resources.

- Future-proof yourself for a digital and AI-driven economy by learning to create value independently.

- Establish your financial and entrepreneurial foundation at an early age to support you throughput entire life.

Being born poor is not a choice, as you inherit the wealth of your parents mindset and sum of their accomplishments. Dying poor however - is. If you are not making decisions that generate wealth for you, your family, and your society, you are not doing it right. Identifying a viable business idea is a chance to grow, contribute, and create value. This book shares unconventional truths that I have learned in my life, most of which are seldom imparted to you while you are students. The ideas I share here are shared to help you build competitive, comparative, and collaborative advantages in a complex digital world filled with opportunities waiting for those of you prepared to seize them.

Although this book offers practical guidance for students studying on every continent, two universal truths remain: no-pain no-gain and the person at the top of the mountain did not fall there. Commitment and effort matter.

Peter J. Middlebrook

What you hold in your hands is a cheat sheet for thinking differently about your student years, your choices, and the opportunities that exist even when you think you have none.

2. How to Read This Book

A Shortcut to Building Personal Wealth

This book is structured around a simple logic. Before you can build an income stream (or streams) that align with your aspirations, choose a strategy, or launch any of the ideas in the later chapters, you will need a greater understanding about what drives and shapes your ambition. That is why the book begins with the most important questions you will ever ask yourself: who are you, what do you want, what do you value, and what are your core motivations? These questions shape everything that follows, and they will influence the decisions you take long after you close this book.

Do not rush past these questions as they are foundational to you. Many of you may be tempted to just jump straight to the chapters about how to make money, but money without direction becomes noise and distraction. If you take this seriously, spend a week with the questions in Chapter 3 below, thinking deeply about the real you. Think about the life you want to live, the work that energizes you, and the goals that matter before you die. Your answers will become the compass that guides every choice you make in this book

As you discover the authentic you, keep reminding yourself that you are born with nothing, spend much of your life chasing everything, and leave with nothing regardless. On your deathbed, you will almost certainly remember the people you loved and the difference you made, not the cars and houses, the computers and watches accumulated along the way. Income, like food, exists simply to sustain you as you live your life.

Once you understand the real or more authentic you, the next step is learning how to see abundance. That means training your mind to notice opportunities instead of problems, to observe needs instead of obstacles, and to recognize the patterns that show where value is hiding. Changing the way you see the world is a mindset shift, and it takes time. Students who learn to see abundance always outpace those who think in scarcity. Read that chapter slowly, sit with it, and let it challenge the way you currently view your life.

From there, the book focuses on practical tools and checklists. You will learn understand the true nature of business and money, and how to identify investment opportunities by solving problems and servicing other people's needs. You will look closely at income types, business models, and the difference between working for money and building something that lets money work for you. Each chapter builds on the last, with each being designed to add a new layer of understanding, until you finally reach the point where you can design your own income strategy.

You can jump ahead if you want to, but the real power of this book lies in reading it in order. The graphic on the next page shows the logic. Start with who you are. Understand what you want. Recognize what you already have. See what you can do. Identify where the opportunity is. Choose the income types that fit you. Decide on the strategy you will use based on your own rather unique starting point. Build something small. Improve it. Scale it. Then create a future that reflects the person you want to become.

I encourage you to treat this book like a toolkit for your mind. Use it to think, to build, and to design your next steps in life with intention. Read it slowly. Reflect often. Your goal is not to rush through content but to emerge from it with a personal strategy that fits your identity, your strengths, and your ambitions. If you do that, the final chapter will not be the end of a book. It will be the beginning of your future.

BUILD YOUR OWN STRATEGY

FIGURE OUT WHO YOU ARE

↓

MOVE FROM A SCARCITY TO ABUNDANCE MINDSET

↓

UNDERSTAND THE NATURE OF MONEY

↓

UNDERSTAND THE NATURE OF BUSINESS

↓

SEE WHERE YOU FIT IN

↓

IDENTIFY OPPORTUNITIES

↓

DEVELOP YOUR PLAN

↓

TAKE ACTION

↓

CREATE THE FUTURE

3. UNDERSTANDING THE REAL YOU

Overcoming the Hidden Architecture Shaping Your Life

Have you ever felt like your life is on autopilot? You are drifting in a direction you never consciously chose? Days pass, choices accumulate, and somehow you find yourself traveling along the path of least resistance rather than the path of your own design and destiny. It is a quiet slide, guided more by habits that are both inherited and learned, expectation, and the social context around you than by any deliberate act of self-creation.

I have only felt like this during one period of my life – caught between aspiration to being a musician and about to enter the University of Northumbria in the UK (then a polytechnic). I remember distinctly someone asking me who I wanted to be, and I didn't have a damn clue. That I could not answer shocked me deeply – who was I, why was I here, why was my future not screaming out like a sunlit highway in front of me? This brief phase of uncertainty however was necessary - the silence before the storm if you like – and answering the questions I pose for you here should make all the difference.

Most of you probably do not even notice your lack of direction happening. In fact, you may never question it at all. You are who you are, because the apple never grew far from the tree! It often takes years to realize that your life has been shaped by parents (rich and poor), societal norms or circumstance, not your own design. While your

16

environment shapes you substantially, in many ways, lack of guidance by parents and the state on personal finances acts as a brake on your future. Breaking that pattern begins with a single step, the decision to understand who you truly are (the authentic you) and to steer your future with purpose rather than momentum or drift – towards your very own personal objective.

At the heart of this book, and of your ability to build wealth while you are still a student, lies an inward journey. You need to identify what genuinely moves you. It may not be money at all - it never was my primary motivator either. What lights your fire? What energizes you? Being unmistakably clear about this allows you to say no to investments that do not interest you, and to give a clear green light to ideas that make you feel you are moving in the direction you were always meant to travel.

You know you are drifting when every day feels like Groundhog Day, powered by habit rather than Red Bull or oxygen. Remember, if you are not having fun, you are not doing it right. This is the moment to pay attention to your own curiosity, to the pull that draws you toward certain ideas, and to the surge of energy that appears when you work on something that genuinely matters to you. Alongside this comes a quieter belief, often overlooked, that your future belongs entirely to you and nobody else. You do not need to live your life at someone else's expense.

In 2000, when in Ethiopia, I shared a private breakfast with Bob Marley's wife Rita. Over toast and coffee, she uttered one of Bob's most enduring lines: *"Free yourself from mental slavery, for none but yourself can free your mind."*[2] This phrase should remind you that each second, minute, hour, day, week, month and year belongs solely to you. How you spend it is your choice, nobody else. So, own it.

In identifying who you are, just remember that many events in the future are certainly going to happen, so treat them as if they are already here. For example, you live in the digital age. Be aware that AI will increasingly remove many of the repetitive, low-value tasks that drain time and distract you from your real strengths. While there is a huge demand for blue-collar jobs, make sure that the choices you make now make sense in say 5 to 10 years-time from now. Embracing AI

---

[2] Marley, B. (1980) *Redemption Song*. On: *Uprising* [Album]. Tuff Gong Records.

early could also allow you to operate in your authentic genius zone, focusing on the ideas, decisions, and creative instincts that genuinely reflect who you are. AI, if used well, can help you make better decisions.

When you understand yourself clearly, your time, effort, and ambition stop scattering. They align, strengthen each other, and build momentum that allows you to create wealth, confidence, and a life of your own design far earlier than most people ever dream possible. When you understand yourself, and your wider purpose in life, you commit every moment to that outcome.

Recognize The Hidden Architecture Shaping Your Life

Are you your own architect, or has your life been constructed (even lovingly) by parents, friends and / or society at large? Do you know who you are, what you want, and how to achieve it? Do you know how to spend but not to earn, how to consume, but not to produce, how to labor, but not to invest?

For most of you, many of the decisions taken in your life have not been taken by you. The name you were given, your nationality, your religion, family expectations, and even your financial circumstances were all set long before you had a say in anything.

Your parents and the people closest to you become the reference points for what you believe is normal. If everyone around you works a low paid nine to five job, that becomes the horizon of what feels possible. If your parents were investment bankers, entrepreneurs, or creators, you would grow up with a completely different sense of time, money, risk, and how to see opportunity. Your environment becomes the invisible architecture of your thinking.

These familiar forces shape the edges of your world and steer you toward a path that feels safe but may not be yours at all. To evolve beyond your current realm of influence, you need to better understand the rules for the game of life, to be a better player and even a rule maker.

The Moment You Take Back Control

Conventional logic tells you that life does not begin until after graduation.

Rich Student. Poor Student.

You follow the system, take on debt, do a few side gigs, and only start your economic life once you have your bachelor's degree. You scan the job market, take the first job that comes along, stay there far too long, and soon you have kids and a mortgage. The word mortgage in essence means 'death pledge 'in French, following which the cost of kids, accommodation, food and another cycle of education mean you simply never achieve the escape velocity to break out and be financially independent.

This book outlines a fundamentally different architecture, allowing you to upgrade your 'mental software', following which you will view time, money, investment and risks fundamentally differently. Taking back control means that your 'environment' is a product of you, you are not a product of the overall environment. To achieve this however, you will need to ask and answer deep and searching questions, which I provide below.

I propose that you begin investing in your own financial independence not after your education, but alongside it. Yes, it is like building the plane while flying it, but students have something most adults do not: a safety net of family, friends and the wider system around them. Your student years are the ideal time to experiment, take risks and make mistakes. Far better to learn your lessons now than when you have children, a mortgage and responsibilities that leave no room for error.

The ability to see money, time and opportunity differently from everyone around you is the beginning of everything.

Why Most Students Drift

Many students select courses they will never use later in life. Perhaps you did not know the real you when you chose, and as you evolved, you realized that what you are studying is no longer your first choice.

You drift into studying subjects that do not match either your authentic self or ambitions. Only a small number, usually mature students who have gained a clearer sense of self through real life experience, end up finding the most optimal direction to follow. They choose subjects that are more closely aligned to their identity, rather than the assuming the identity that society tries to impose on them.

If you know who you are early in life, you can build the rest of your life with speed, precision, and purpose.

How Did I Figure Out Who I Was?

I always knew who I was, but it was not until I was 15 years of age - watching the famine unfold in Ethiopia – that I was introduced to my greater purpose.

Seeing children starve stirred something deep inside me. It made me realize that dedicating my life to human rights mattered far more than chasing anything rooted in ego. Only then did I look back at the life I had been working towards, being a professional footballer or musician. I loved all of it, and I threw myself fully into every pursuit, but that moment revealed what truly mattered to me – human dignity in the face of adversity.

That moment was like a bomb going off in the right place, from which all other decisions I have subsequently taken have been conditioned and shaped.

That moment is why I left England to travel to more than 100 countries and to work in more than 50. That moment is why – and despite having no education - I completed my bachelor's in environmental studies from the University of Northumbria in Newcastle, and my PhD at the University of Durham in Northern England. Some 14 years after seeing the famine on TV, I managed to skillfully position myself as a key advisor with the European Union and the British government in Ethiopia. It was a deliberate and specific choice, rooted in the country that helped shape the beginning of my adult life and much of the work I have undertaken.

Today, I am the CEO of two companies: a consulting group based in the Middle East advising governments, multilaterals and bilateral agencies and the United Nations globally, and a company in the United States designing and delivering affordable shelter and housing for refugees and homeless people.

In discovering who I truly was, I also learned a hard truth: ideas alone are not enough. You need money and resources to achieve your life's mission. The wealth I have created through business has allowed me to be myself fully, to deliver the work I believe in, and to build the financial foundation from which many of the lessons and ideas in this book have emerged.

Stripping Away the Layers

If you are living inside someone else's architecture and fear that you only know how to spend and consume, then you need to strip away your current avatar and peel back the layers to find the authentic you.

Here is a deep and searching exercise for you. Set aside your name, your social and economic background, the community that shaped you, your resume, and every piece of identity you inherited rather than chose. Strip all of it away. Even if it leaves you feeling exposed, the person who remains in that moment is the real you.

That person, the one you may barely know, holds your natural instincts, your boldest ideas, the most authentic version of you, and the seed of the life you are meant to plant, nurture and grow.

Questions You Need to Ask Yourself Before You Start

Before you begin building wealth, a business or even a direction for your life, you need clarity about who you are and what you want. These questions are designed to pull you away from noise, pressure and expectation, and bring you back to your deeper instincts. They force you to look at what energizes you, what you are naturally good at, the kind of life you want to live, and what you are willing to work for when things become difficult. They also free your imagination by asking what you would do if failure were impossible.

Taken together, these questions reveal the foundations of your identity and the raw material you will use to build your future as a student and future entrepreneur.

Table 2.	THE FIVE QUESTIONS THAT SHAPE YOUR FUTURE
Your Question	**Things to Consider**
Who is the authentic you?	Look beneath your name, your upbringing, expectations, ego and the history you inherited. Identify the person who exists when all labels, identities and external influences are stripped away.
What single goal must you achieve before you die?	If you had to choose only one life outcome, the one that is non-negotiable, name it clearly. This becomes your compass for every major decision ahead.

Table 2.	THE FIVE QUESTIONS THAT SHAPE YOUR FUTURE
Your Question	**Things to Consider**
What are your core skills and interests?	Identify the abilities and passions that make you feel alive, energized and fully yourself. These reveal the work you are naturally built to pursue and excel at.
Do you intend to work in the public sector or the private sector?	Clarify whether your future lies in government, not-for-profit work, or in private enterprise. This determines the environments, opportunities and financial pathways you will prioritize.
How much money do you need to live well and achieve your goal?	Decide the level of income or wealth required for you to live a healthy, productive life and meet your single life goal. The clearer the number, the clearer the path.

How to Approach This Exercise

Before you move deeper into this book, you need greater clarity about who you are, what you want, and what your life is aiming toward.

These five questions are not designed to be answered quickly or casually. You should sit somewhere quiet, take out a notebook, and commit real time to writing your answers. Revisit them over days and weeks. Let the answers evolve. These are not trick questions, but they are life-defining ones. They determine whether you will live as a passive consumer of other people's plans or as an active producer shaping your own future. Your responses will guide every step that follows in this book, including which financial activities, entrepreneurial paths, and personal strategies are best aligned with the person you truly are and the life you want to build.

In answering these questions, look at the simple guidance notes below, knowing that true answers to these questions may cause you to question the path you are on.

Table 3.	GUIDANCE NOTES FOR THE FIVE QUESTIONS
Look beneath your name, your upbringing, your family's expectations, your ego and the history you inherited. Identify the person who remains when all external layers are stripped away.	
Identify the single life outcome that is completely non-negotiable. Reduce all your ambitions to the one goal you must achieve before you die.	
List the skills and interests that make you feel alive, energized and fully engaged. Look for the overlap between what you're good at and what excites you.	

Table 3.	GUIDANCE NOTES FOR THE FIVE QUESTIONS
Clarify whether your future lies in government or not-for-profit work, or in private enterprise. This determines the financial and professional path ahead.	
Estimate how much money you need each year to live a healthy, productive life. Define the level of income or assets required to support the one goal you've chosen.	

Rich or Poor?

A rich student is someone who has taken the time to understand their direction in life and refuses to wait for formal education to end before building their future. They start laying foundations early, using their school years, their college years, and even the years before university to experiment, earn, invest, develop skills, and shape their economic independence in parallel with their studies.

A poor student is not poor in character or ambition, but simply someone who has not yet figured out what they want, who drifts from subject to subject, accepts whatever outcome appears, and tends to rely on the traditional path of waiting until graduation before beginning adult life. There is nothing wrong with being an employee — serving in the corporate world or public sector, working in education, healthcare, or government is honorable and vital, and society only functions because people commit to these roles. I spent twenty years earning well as an international civil servant before I decided to be clearer about generating wealth, to fund my ideas and provide me the monetary capacity to say 'no', if asked to do something that is fundamentally against my authentic nature.

But for those who want financial freedom, and for those who want to avoid the standard sequence of mortgages, marriage, children, and debt dictating their choices, these questions become essential. They allow you to design your life deliberately, rather than inherit one by default, and to build your financial independence early rather than late.

Vicious Student-to-Life Cycle

This cycle shows how many young people move from education into adulthood without ever gaining financial independence. They follow the system, take on debt, finish their degree, grab the first job that appears, stay there too long, then accumulate obligations like kids, housing and the infamous mortgage, which literally means *death pledge*. Rising costs and continuous responsibility drain time, energy and money, trapping them in a loop where escape velocity is never reached. The cycle becomes self-reinforcing, creating adults who are always running but never breaking free.

Virtuous Student-to-Life Cycle

This cycle shows how a student who knows who they are and what they want can move from education into adulthood with clarity, purpose and growing financial independence. Instead of waiting for life to begin after graduation, they build their future in parallel with their studies. They identify their strengths, choose a direction early, and use their student years to learn, experiment, earn, and invest. They avoid the trap of drifting into the first available job and instead pursue opportunities that match their long-term goals. By creating small streams of income, learning to sell or build something of value, and developing a business or investment that earns even while they sleep, they gain early momentum. Over time, their confidence, skills and resources compound. The cycle becomes self-reinforcing, creating young adults who are not trapped by debt or circumstance but are steadily moving toward freedom, choice and financial independence.

Both cycles are provided in Figure 1 below, to stimulate your imagination in identifying where you are, and which direction to go.

Figure 1: VICIOUS & VIRTUOUS STUDENT- LIFE CYCLES

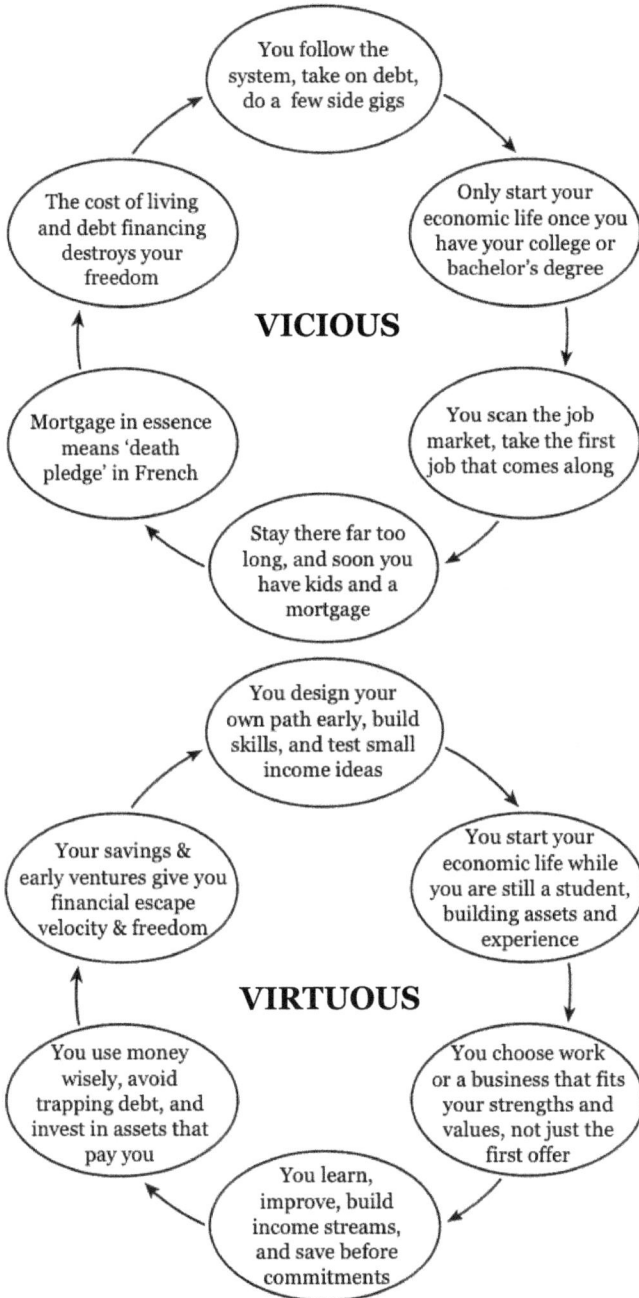

VICIOUS

- You follow the system, take on debt, do a few side gigs
- Only start your economic life once you have your college or bachelor's degree
- You scan the job market, take the first job that comes along
- Stay there far too long, and soon you have kids and a mortgage
- Mortgage in essence means 'death pledge' in French
- The cost of living and debt financing destroys your freedom

VIRTUOUS

- You design your own path early, build skills, and test small income ideas
- You start your economic life while you are still a student, building assets and experience
- You choose work or a business that fits your strengths and values, not just the first offer
- You learn, improve, build income streams, and save before commitments
- You use money wisely, avoid trapping debt, and invest in assets that pay you
- Your savings & early ventures give you financial escape velocity & freedom

4. LEARNING TO SEE ABUNDANCE

When You Learn How to See, Opportunity Abounds

Money and wealth are created by serving other people, either by providing services or selling products they want. Your primary task is to identify things that people need but do not yet have, then find a way to provide those things. You do not always need to produce anything yourself. You can source, supply, or resell. With global e-commerce platforms, you can sell to anyone, anywhere, at any time. But your most immediate marketplace is right in front of you. Your university, college, or school is full of unmet needs. Your fellow students are a live test audience for what people will pay for. Begin by asking what they lack, what frustrates them, what they need urgently, and what you can access more easily than they can. This is the foundation of entrepreneurship, and it is a route you can start today, not after you graduate.

Learning to see abundance begins with a shift in attention. Opportunity is everywhere once you train your mind to notice needs, gaps, and frustrations others overlook. Money flows to those who solve problems for people, either through services or through products that make life easier. You can source, package, improve, resell, or simply connect people to what they already want. Your campus remains the ideal place to test your ideas, a living micro economy where students are busy, stressed, and often lacking simple essentials they are willing to pay for. Your task is to observe closely, ask smart questions, and offer simple solutions with real value.

Today, artificial intelligence amplifies this way of seeing. It allows you to spot patterns, trends and gaps far faster than previous generations. With a few prompts, AI can analyze markets, scan competitors, summaries hundreds of comments, or test the early shape of an idea. AI does not replace your ability to observe, it strengthens it. It helps you see connections, problems and possibilities that would otherwise remain invisible. Once you train yourself to look outward with curiosity, AI becomes the lens that sharpens your vision.

Figure Out How to Make Money While You Are Sleeping

Making money while you are asleep is the cleanest test of whether you are building wealth or just trading hours. It forces you to create something that earns money without your constant effort. That could be a product listed online, a simple service running on automation, a digital file that sells repeatedly, or a small campus business that operates even when you are not present. It could be assets that gain in value, driven by market demand.

The principle is straightforward. You need something circulating in the world that keeps generating value long after you have switched off the lights. Once you build that, you move from surviving on effort to building real independence.

The Scarcity to Abundance Mindset

The contrast between a scarcity mindset and an abundance mindset is one of the most powerful dividers between those who shape the future and those who merely adapt to it. The concept itself is not new. The language of scarcity and abundance was popularised by Stephen R. Covey, who described how people with a scarcity mindset view life as a finite pie, while those with an abundance mindset believe that opportunity, creativity and value can be expanded rather than competed over (Covey, 1989).

This book builds on that insight and applies it directly to the realities students face today. A scarcity mindset focuses attention on limits, obstacles and perceived disadvantages. It leads people to wait, to defer action, and to assume that opportunity is reserved for others. An abundance mindset works in the opposite direction. It trains attention on unmet needs, inefficiencies and gaps, and asks how value might be created where none appears to exist.

Students who adopt an abundance mindset are more likely to experiment, to innovate, and to act early. Rather than seeing constraints as reasons to stand still, they treat them as raw material for solutions. This shift in perspective is not about optimism or positive thinking. It is about learning to see the world as malleable, shaped by human action, rather than as a fixed system to be endured.

People like Jeff Bezos, Elon Musk, and many others have trained themselves to see abundance everywhere. Where most people see nothing special, they see the seed of the next solution. They notice friction, inconvenience, or unmet demand, and immediately ask how many people have that same problem and whether a new product or service could fix it. This mindset shift is the starting point of wealth creation.

A scarcity mindset says nothing can be changed, opportunities are limited, and life is fixed in place. It leaves you believing that your circumstances define your future and that the world is already full. An abundance mindset works the opposite way. It starts with the belief that new ideas, new solutions, and new businesses are waiting to be discovered. When something goes wrong, or when you do not have what you need, the question becomes not "why is this happening to me," but "how many others suffer from the same issue and could I design a way out of it."

We are often bound by the limits of our own imagination. The challenge for every student is to stop thinking like everyone else and start seeing problems as gateways. The Chinese character for danger is made up of two ideas, crisis and opportunity existing together. In the same moment you feel stuck, exposed, or stressed, there is often a parallel opening for a new idea. The most successful students lean into that opening rather than retreat from it.

Mark Zuckerberg, whatever your view of Facebook, illustrates this perfectly. He saw that students wanted a way to connect and share information with people they could not reach easily. The problem was simple; people wanted a network. The solution became one of the largest platforms in the world. Abundance thinking operates exactly like this, look for the human need first, then build the bridge to meet it.

A scarcity mindset says the world is dull, nothing can change, and everything important has already been done. It is not true. If life feels boring, it means your curiosity is asleep. The moment you begin noticing problems instead of skipping past them, the world becomes a map of possibilities waiting to be explored. Students who adopt this mindset will always have more doors to walk through than those who assume the world has already run out of opportunities.

How to Identify and Invest in Abundance Solutions

Not everyone sees opportunities in the same way. Part of this comes from acumen, intellect, desire, and passion, but most of it comes from training your mind to look differently at the world around you. Every errand you run, every essay you write, every school event you join, every sports match you watch, and every graduation you attend is full of unmet needs. Begin asking one simple question wherever you go, what is it that people want that they do not have? Once this question becomes automatic, the world starts revealing gaps that most people never notice.

Think about the inventions you love today. Almost all of them started as simple frustrations. Someone thought, why is this so difficult, and realized millions of others felt exactly the same way. The person who created the solution was not always the smartest person in the room, but they were the one who paid attention. Abundance thinking works exactly like this. The shift from an employee mindset to a producer or business owner mindset begins when you stop assuming the world is already complete and start looking for the problems that nobody has solved yet. Many of the most successful student businesses begin with simple products or services that required more observation than brilliance.

When you identify a repeated frustration, ask how many people face it, whether it happens daily or weekly, and how much easier life becomes if the problem disappears. These questions turn ordinary moments into investment clues. Once you begin spotting patterns, you can start experimenting with small, low-cost solutions. Some will fail, some will work, and each attempt builds your sense of where real opportunity hides.

Practical Steps to Shift from Consumer to Producer

- Start carrying a small notebook or a notes app for recording every problem you notice, however trivial.

- Ask immediately how many others face the same issue when you experience inconvenience.

- Look for solutions that already exist and ask whether you could improve, simplify, or localize them.

- Study the habits of your fellow students, especially during stress points like exams, deadlines, and travel.

- Analyze your own spending. Everything you buy is evidence of someone else solving a need you had.

- Spend one hour a week researching simple products that became global successes from small beginnings.

- Build one tiny solution every month, even if it is crude, to strengthen your problem-solving muscles.

- Observe marketplaces around you, campus shops, online stores, student forums, and ask what people repeatedly search for but cannot easily get.

- Surround yourself with people who think creatively and challenge you to question your assumptions.

- Focus on value creation first, income second. Money follows solutions, not ideas that only excite you.

Be Inspired by Real World Examples

Seeing abundance means recognizing problems others accept as normal and then crafting solutions that others hadn't considered. Below are student-era examples of people who did exactly that: they noticed a gap, built something to fill it, and turned that into real value. Use these to spark your own thinking about what you might build.

Rich Student. Poor Student.

These real-world examples (See Table 4 below) show that abundance does not need to be complex or formal. Most opportunities begin as small, simple solutions that earn $10, $20, $50, or $100 a day. The key is not the size of the idea but the mindset behind it. Students with an abundance mindset notice problems others ignore, design practical fixes, and benefit financially because they acted when nobody else did. From campus frustrations to community gaps to global needs, the pattern is always the same, see the opportunity, build the solution, and capture the value.

Chapter 9, One Hundred Ideas for Student Businesses, provides a wide range of abundance driven ideas that any student can explore and start immediately.

Table 4.	PRACTICAL EXAMPLES FROM THE REAL WORLD		
Name	**Problem Identified**	**Solution Created**	**Result / Scale**
Blaine Vess (Student Brands)	Students needed better access to essays, study notes, flashcards.	Founded Student Brands while still in college, built a network of educational websites (StudyMode, flashcards etc.)	Acquired for approx. US$58.5 million in 2017.
Kimeshan Naidoo & Diego Fanara (Unibuddy)	Prospective students lacked authentic peer-to-peer info about universities.	Founded a platform where students and alumni chat with prospective students	Global institution partnerships (500+), millions of messages exchanged.
Founders of WayUp (Liz Wessel & JJ Fliegelman)	Recent grads and students lacked tailored job/internship marketplace.	Created WayUp to match students and recent grads with jobs/internships.	Raised multi-million funding; large network of employers and users.
Founders of Uniplaces (Miguel Amaro, Mariano Kostelec, Ben Grech)	Students studying abroad struggled to find safe, trusted accommodation.	Built Uniplaces, an online marketplace for student accommodation.	Students from 140+ countries booked through platform; raised major funding.

Table 4. PRACTICAL EXAMPLES FROM THE REAL WORLD			
Name	**Problem Identified**	**Solution Created**	**Result / Scale**
Founders of Portfolium (Adam Markowitz, Royce Rowan, Daniel Marashlian)	Graduates struggled to showcase academic project work to employers in meaningful way.	Created Portfolium, platform allowing students to upload project-work portfolios for employers.	Raised seed funding, acquired later.
Christoph Koenig	As a BSc student, saw the opportunity to turn his student work into a startup.	Founded a startup during his bachelor program (Clay and...) in management.	Became startup founder by end of degree.
Michael Nixon	Teenage student saw kids lacked engaging STEM kits in Australia.	Founded EduKits / The Amazing Annoyatron for kids to learn coding and electronics.	Won national awards, exported product to multiple countries.
Hopkins Consulting Agency (student-run at Johns Hopkins University)	University research labs and inventors lacked affordable student-run consulting support.	Students founded HCA offering business-plan preparation and tech commercialization consulting.	Operates as student enterprise, real clients, real revenue
Frederick W. Smith (pre-FedEx student idea)	Overnight package shipping was inefficient and fragmented.	While a student at Yale, he developed the concept for an air-freight overnight service (which became FedEx)	FedEx now a global logistics giant.
(Bonus) A student project example: CodeLab, University of São Paulo	Student community lacked structured hackathon & learning ecosystem.	Built CodeLab initiative to create regular hackathons, engaged student community and enterprise innovation.	15 competitions over five years; shows scaling of student-driven initiative.

5. BECOMING A STUDENT ENTREPRENEUR

From Personal Scarcity to Abundance

For most students, if someone hands you 1,000 dollars, 2,000 dollars, or even 5,000 dollars, your instinct is to think about what you can spend it on.

Most people immediately imagine buying a new phone, a better laptop, or some other shiny but rapidly depreciating item. They choose things that lose value the moment they leave the store instead of choosing something that, at the very least, keeps pace with inflation or, ideally, appreciates over time.

Most people are taught to be consumers, not producers. Employees think about spending. Even many self-employed people think about spending. Investors think differently. They ask a better question: *How can I maximize the rate of return on this money?* The moment you stop treating money as something to spend and start treating it as something to deploy, you shift from consumption to creation. That single shift in thinking is the foundation of becoming a student entrepreneur.

As Warren Buffett famously advises, 'Rule No. 1: Never lose money. Rule No. 2: Never forget Rule No. 1.' This principle captures Buffett's long-standing emphasis on capital preservation. Recovering from significant losses is far harder than achieving steady gains, which is why protecting downside risk sits at the core of his investment philosophy (Dolan, 2025).

Buffett has also repeatedly described wealth-building as a process similar to a snowball rolling downhill. The longer it rolls, and the more consistently it gathers material, the larger it becomes. In this view, time and compounding matter more than speed or brilliance. Starting early, remaining patient, and allowing returns to accumulate year after year is what ultimately transforms modest beginnings into substantial wealth. This analogy is so central to Buffett's thinking that it gave its name to his authorized biography, *The Snowball* (Schroeder, 2008).

The first rule of investing is simple: preserve your capital. Never lose money. Your minimum goal is to ensure that whatever you invest in, at the very least, keeps pace with inflation. And remember, inflation eats the value of your money. Every year that prices rise faster than the interest you earn, the real purchasing power of your savings shrinks. Leaving your money in a basic bank account with a very low interest rate might feel safe, but from an investment point of view it is simply watching your wealth erode slowly. Inflation is the silent tax on every saver, and if your returns do not match or exceed it, you are going backwards financially, even if the number in your bank account stays the same.

Are Student Entrepreneurs Born or Made?

The word *entrepreneur* comes from the French *entreprendre*, meaning *to undertake, to initiate*, or *to begin something*. The term was adopted into English because no other word captured the combination of vision, initiative, responsibility and risk-taking required to build something from nothing. An entrepreneur is someone who sees opportunity (abundance) where others see routine, someone who takes responsibility for creating value rather than waiting for value to be handed to them. Entrepreneurs do not simply work inside a system, they design systems, improve them, or break them entirely to build better ones.

A student entrepreneur applies this mindset long before graduation. Instead of simply taking a loan, spending it, and emerging with debt, a student entrepreneur thinks carefully about the assets they already possess; time, energy, networks, skills, curiosity, creativity, and the safety net that university life provides. They ask different questions. What can I build? What can I sell? How can I use what I have to generate income? How can I ensure that I do not leave education poorer, but stronger, more capable, and already operating in the real economy? A student entrepreneur aims not only to avoid debt, but ideally to lay an economic foundation while still studying that will carry them into post-graduation life with confidence and momentum.

So, are entrepreneurs born or made? The answer is both. Some people are born with a personality that naturally leans toward initiative, independence, curiosity, and risk-taking. They feel restless inside the confines of normality and often show these traits from an early age. But entrepreneurship is also a discipline that can be taught, strengthened, and learned. Anyone willing to read books like this, to ask themselves sharper questions, to train their mind to look at the world differently from the average employee, and to cultivate the habits of creation rather than consumption, can become an entrepreneur. Natural talent helps, but mindset, practice, and perspective matter far more.

Entrepreneurship is not a gift reserved for the few. It is a way of seeing the world, and anyone who chooses to adopt that way of seeing can begin the journey.

How Does a Student Entrepreneur See the World?

A student entrepreneur does not see the world the way most people do. Where the average student sees routines, inconveniences, annoyances, or background noise, the student entrepreneur sees patterns, unmet needs, inefficiencies, gaps, friction points, and—most importantly—opportunities. They train their mind to ask a simple, life-changing question wherever they go: What is the problem here, and how many people have the same problem?

When everyone else is looking *at* the world, they are looking *into* it. They observe, analyze, question, and imagine. They notice the things others overlook and then have the courage and energy to build or provide something that solves the problem. That is the root of entrepreneurial thinking: not genius, not luck, but attention, imagination, and action.

35

Below are practical examples of how a student entrepreneur sees opportunities everywhere:

Examples of How a Student Entrepreneur Thinks

- End-of-year student move-outs leave piles of unwanted furniture and appliances. *Entrepreneurial view:* These are assets to sell, refurbish, store, or rent to incoming students.

- Students panic about shipping their belongings home for summer. *Entrepreneurial view:* Offer organized packing, storage, and group shipping services.

- International students pay high prices for basic items after arrival. *Entrepreneurial view:* Pre-assembled "arrival kits" with bedding, utensils, and essentials.

- Libraries get crowded during exam season. *Entrepreneurial view:* Create or rent alternative quiet study spaces, or build a booking app.

- Classmates struggle with printing assignments at midnight. *Entrepreneurial view:* Late-night dorm-based printing service with small delivery fees.

- Students constantly forget chargers, adapters, or headphones. *Entrepreneurial view:* Small vending machines or a dorm-based rental/exchange system.

- Student societies always need logos, posters, and quick designs. *Entrepreneurial view:* Fast-turnaround graphic design service using AI or Upwork.

- Lectures and tutorials produce mountains of notes. *Entrepreneurial view:* Compile and sell high-quality study guides or summaries.

- Campus gyms get overcrowded at peak times. *Entrepreneurial view:* Offer off-peak personal training, group classes, or outdoor boot camps.

- Local restaurants struggle to reach student customers. *Entrepreneurial view:* Create a student-focused discount card or food-delivery partnership.

- Students constantly lose keys, IDs, and wallets. *Entrepreneurial view:* Offer custom RFID tags, trackers, or a lost-and-found concierge system.

- Clubs and teams need photography or videography for events. *Entrepreneurial view:* Become the campus photographer, videographer, or editor.

- Dorm rooms are bland and poorly decorated. *Entrepreneurial view:* Sell low-cost décor bundles or offer quick makeover services.

- Freshers (new students) feel overwhelmed and uninformed. *Entrepreneurial view:* Build a guidebook, onboarding service, or "buddy" mentorship program.

- Students pay high prices for textbooks they only use once. *Entrepreneurial view:* Buy, rent, or resell textbooks as a micro-business.

- Clubs, sports teams, and societies need coordinated merchandise. *Entrepreneurial view:* Provide a custom merch or print-on-demand service.

- Students often have unused skills they never monetize. *Entrepreneurial view:* Create a skill-exchange marketplace where students hire each other.

A student entrepreneur sees the world as a living marketplace. Every complaint is data. Every inconvenience is a gap. Every repeated frustration is a business waiting to happen. They don't ask, *"Why is this happening to me?"* They ask, *"How many others have this problem, and what can I build to solve it?"* This is the mindset that separates those who wait for opportunity from those who create it.

How to Become a Student Entrepreneur

Before you can build anything in the outside world, you need clarity on the inside. That is why you answered the five questions earlier: Who is the authentic you? What single goal must you achieve before you die? What skills and interests define you? Which sector fits your identity? And how much money do you need to live well and achieve your purpose?

These answers are not philosophical exercises. They are your blueprint. They tell you what direction you should take, how you should think, and where you should look for opportunities. Without this internal compass, you will copy what others do instead of creating your own path. With clarity, you stop drifting and start choosing, designing, and building.

Entrepreneurs themselves come in many forms, but they tend to fall into three broad archetypes. Some are gamechangers, people who reshape the rules entirely and refuse to accept life as it is presented to them. Others are innovators, constantly spotting gaps, improving what already exists, and imagining new possibilities before anyone else sees them. And then there are the hustlers, the relentless doers who outwork everyone, turning small opportunities into real momentum through persistence and determination. Every entrepreneur carries elements of all three. Your task is to recognize which one you lean toward today and which traits you must strengthen to build the life you want.

The moment you know who you are and what you want, the world looks different. Problems stop feeling like inconveniences and begin to appear as raw materials for solutions. Needs become markets. Complaints become data. Frustrations become opportunities. You stop asking "Why is this happening to me?" and start asking "How many people have this same problem, and what simple solution would make their life easier?"

Entrepreneurship is a skill, but it begins with perception. You train yourself to see what others ignore, to think beyond the obvious, and to notice patterns that repeat across days, weeks, seasons, and student life cycles. Many students wait for inspiration or a "big idea," but that is not how real entrepreneurs begin. They start by paying attention. They look closer. They ask better questions.

Table 5 provides a cheat sheet for wannabe student entrepreneurs, a practical guide you can use every day to train your mind to see abundance instead of scarcity, to recognize opportunities hiding in plain sight, and to turn problems into pathways for value creation. This is your first real toolkit for thinking like an entrepreneur rather than like an employee.

Table 5.	CHEAT SHEET FOR STUDENT ENTREPRENEURS
Category	**Guiding Questions / Actions**
1. If You Have No Idea Where to Start	▪ Given who you are and what you want, who are *your people*? (Students, internationals, local businesses, online creators?) ▪ What problems do they repeatedly complain about? ▪ Which problems annoy you enough that you would gladly solve them? ▪ What do you already know how to do that others find difficult or boring? ▪ If you had to earn $100 by Friday without getting a job, what would you sell or do? **Action:** Write down 3 groups of people, 3 repeated problems, and 3 things you can already do. The intersection is your starting map.
2. How to See the World Differently	▪ What around me is wasteful, confusing, frustrating, or slow? ▪ How many people experience the same problem? ▪ Is there an existing solution? If yes, why isn't it reaching people? Could I deliver it faster, cheaper, or closer? ▪ If no solution exists, what would a simple version look like? ▪ If I could fix one thing on campus with a magic wand, what would I choose? **Action:** Record at least five problems a day in a notebook or notes app. Don't judge. Collect them.
3. How to Start Seeing	▪ Who exactly has this problem? (Be specific.) ▪ When and where is it worst? (Season, time, place.)

Table 5.	CHEAT SHEET FOR STUDENT ENTREPRENEURS
Category	**Guiding Questions / Actions**
Problems and Solutions	<ul><li>How are people coping with it now? (Workarounds, hacks.)</li><li>Could I organize something? deliver something? rent or share something? design or create something? simplify or bundle something?</li><li>What is the simplest, ugliest version of a solution I can test this week?</li></ul>**Action:** Aim for *testable*, not perfect.
4. How to See Abundance Instead of Scarcity	<ul><li>When something goes wrong, ask: How many others face this exact issue?</li><li>Is this a one-off event, or a repeated cycle?</li><li>If I solve this for myself once, can others use the same solution?</li><li>Could this become a product? a service? a subscription?</li></ul>**Action:** Look for patterns. A one-off problem is unlucky. A repeated problem is a business.
5. Daily Entrepreneurial Questions	<ul><li>Start by noting your own complaints from today, then pick the ones that reveal problems worth solving.</li><li>Pay attention to what others complained about, then spot which frustrations you could remove profitably.</li><li>Recognize the assets you used without thinking, then decide how each one could be turned into value.</li><li>Review where you spent money today, then highlight any cost you could avoid by renting, sharing, or providing the solution yourself.</li><li>Capture one thing you learned today, then choose how to apply it to create more value tomorrow.</li></ul>
6. From Ideas to Action (Small Experiments)	<ul><li>What is the smallest experiment I can run in 48 hours to test interest?</li><li>Could I: put up a poster or post online? ask ten people if they'd pay? sell one version to one person this week?</li><li>If it works, how do I repeat and improve it?</li><li>If it fails, what did I learn about the problem, the customer, or the solution?</li></ul>**Action:** Think like a scientist: test, learn, adjust. The goal is progress, not perfection.

Rich Student. Poor Student.

Whether you are still at school, halfway through your undergraduate degree, or deep into your master's, these questions are your invitation to begin. Treat them as a personal challenge, a test of your curiosity, and a pathway to growth. Go out and observe the world, ask better questions, and experiment with solving real problems. It does not matter whether your first idea earns you twenty dollars or a million dollars. What matters is that you create something, however small, that teaches you how value is built and how problems become opportunities. Each experiment you run becomes part of your escape velocity, lifting you out of the vicious cycle of debt, passive consumption, and preparing to live as an employee in someone else's life. This is the moment you start building a life of your own design.

6. UNDERSTANDING THE NATURE OF BUSINESS

How Business Really Works in the Real World

Once you have identified who you are, what you want, and the opportunities that match your strengths, the next step is to understand the nature of business itself. This short chapter offers a simple primer for students who have never operated in the commercial world. It introduces the full spectrum of business activity, from informal micro-ventures that generate small daily income, to formal registered companies with legal structures, tax obligations, and growth ambitions.

The aim here is not to turn you into a corporate strategist overnight, but to help you think clearly about how businesses actually work: how they compete, differentiate themselves, position ideas in the market, finance their operations, build networks, attract like-minded people, and create brand identity. Once you spot an opportunity that fits you, you must then ask harder questions. Is the market saturated or is there space for a newcomer? Is there a niche entry point others have overlooked? What value would you offer and to whom? Understanding the nature of business will allow you to test your ideas against reality, refine them with purpose, and choose the path that gives you the greatest chance of success.

Artificial intelligence (AI) has shifted this landscape even further. It allows students to launch micro-enterprises with levels of speed, capability and reach that previously required teams, capital, or specialist skills. AI tools reduce startup costs, automate early-stage tasks, improve branding and marketing, and generate insights that help you position your idea more accurately in the market. This means that a single student with a laptop can now build, test, refine and scale a business model that once demanded entire departments. You do not need to replace human judgement, only to amplify it, using AI to remove friction and accelerate the parts of business that slow most people down.

What Do I Mean by the 'Nature' of Business?

When I refer to the *nature* of business, I am talking about the different forms that business can take, the way each type behaves, and the logic that drives how they operate in the real world. Not all businesses are the same. Some are informal, unregistered and run on trust, speed and small daily profits. Others are formal, legally registered entities with tax obligations, regulations, employees and structured financial models. Some businesses rely on personal skill, others on systems, processes, branding, technology or teams. Understanding this spectrum helps you recognize where your potential ideas might fit and what they would require in order to succeed!

Once you see the different layers of business clearly (how value is created, how money flows, how markets behave, and how competitors fight for attention) you can test your own ideas with far greater accuracy. You begin asking better questions: Is this an informal hustle or a scalable venture? Does this market favor small operators or only larger structured firms? What legal or financial tools would I need? How much effort versus return could I expect?

Core Categories and Characteristics

Before you choose where your idea fits, you need to understand the landscape of business itself. A business can begin as something very small, informal and flexible, something you run from your dorm room with little more than your phone and your time. If it works in your university, it might work in other universities, and if it works across campuses, it might work beyond universities altogether. Many great companies began exactly this way.

But seeing the opportunity is only half the picture. The other half is understanding the risks. Most small ventures fail—not because the founders lacked talent, but because they lacked time, capital, structure, market knowledge, or basic business development skills. Some ideas fail because the design is weak, the pricing is wrong, the competition is stronger, or the founder was simply overwhelmed by academic responsibilities. Others fail because the business was never formalized, never adequately financed, never marketed properly, or never taken seriously enough to grow.

Understanding the different types of business (informal hustles, micro-enterprises, formal registered businesses, scalable startups, social ventures) helps you see not just what is possible, but what each path requires. Each comes with different levels of risk, effort, investment, and reward. Table 6 below breaks down these core categories and characteristics so you can understand the terrain clearly before choosing where your idea belongs.

Table 6. THE DIFFERENT FORMS AND NATURE OF BUSINESS			
Type of Business	Description	Typical Features	Examples for Students
Informal Business (Unregistered)	Small-scale, low-barrier activities not formally registered with government. Operates outside tax and regulatory systems.	Cash-based, flexible, fast-moving, easy to start, low risk, low overhead, based on personal trust and networks.	Selling used items, reselling textbooks, tutoring cash-in-hand, dorm cleaning, printing services.
Micro-Enterprise (Semi-Formal)	Very small business sometimes registered but often run by a single person with minimal structure.	May have a simple registration, minimal bookkeeping, small but steady income, slightly more organized than informal hustle.	Freelance design, food prep gigs, small Etsy shop, small-scale event services.
Formal Business (Sole Proprietor / LLC / Company)	Legally recognized entities that must comply with tax	Ability to open business bank accounts, sign contracts, expand	E-commerce business, consultancy service, small

Table 6.	THE DIFFERENT FORMS AND NATURE OF BUSINESS		
Type of Business	**Description**	**Typical Features**	**Examples for Students**
	rules, reporting, and regulations.	operations, hire staff, issue invoices, pay tax.	agency, cleaning company, tech startup.
Non-Profit or Social Enterprise	Mission-driven organization focused on solving a social or environmental problem with or without profit.	Reinforces purpose, may receive grants, donations, or reinvest profits into mission; structured governance.	Campus mentorship program turned NGO, community recycling scheme, education-access platform.
Scalable Business / Startup	High-growth, high-potential venture designed to scale beyond its founder and potentially reach large markets.	Uses technology, systems, or teams to multiply revenue without multiplying costs; may require investment.	Apps, platforms, digital tools, subscription services, student marketplaces.
Franchise or Licensed Model	Business operated using someone else's proven system and brand in exchange for fees or royalties.	Lower risk due to established model, fees to parent company, brand rules to follow.	Student-run College Pro painters, student-owned cleaning franchises, licensed snack carts.

From Informal Hustle to Formal Enterprise

For most students, the earliest income they make will come from small, flexible, informal activities: cash-in-hand tutoring, reselling items, doing design jobs for classmates, printing services, moving services, or baking for events. These are low-risk, low-cost ways to earn money and pay for daily expenses. They sit squarely in the informal sector: easy to start, easy to stop, and requiring almost no administration.

But sometimes a student (or a small group of students) stumbles upon something more meaningful. They identify a problem worth solving, design a solution, and discover that other people are willing to pay for it. What begins as a $500 idea becomes a $2,000 idea. Then $5,000. Then $10,000. At this point the question naturally arises:

When does an informal hustle become a real business?

Formalization is not about bureaucracy for its own sake. It is about recognizing when an idea has outgrown the limits of the informal sector and requires structure, protection, credibility, and the ability to scale. Most great companies began informally—but none stayed that way once they realized what they could become.

When Should You Move from Informal to Formal?

Here are the clearest signals that it is time to register your business, structure it properly, and step into the formal economy:

- **When income becomes regular rather than occasional.** If money flows in every week or month, you are no longer running a side gig—you are running a business.

- **When customers go beyond your immediate circle.** Once strangers pay for your service or product, you need structure, contracts, and protection.

- **When the idea needs more than one person.** If you bring in partners, freelancers, or employees, you need clarity on ownership, roles, and responsibilities.

- **When you want access to finance.** Banks, investors, and grant programs require you to be a registered entity with a tax ID and accounts.

- **When you want to scale beyond your campus.** Growth requires trust—and trust requires legitimacy.

- **When the risks increase.** Legal exposure, customer disputes, and financial liabilities all grow with scale. Formalizing protects you.

Table 7 below provides a simplified global framework to help students understand how informal and formal businesses are classified. These definitions vary slightly by country, but the overall structure is widely used.

Table 7.	HOW BUSINESSES ARE CLASSIFIED INTERNATIONALLY	
Category	**Description**	**Typical Indicators**
Micro-Enterprise	Very small formal or semi-formal business.	1–9 employees; may have a tax ID; basic accounts; extremely small turnover.
Small Enterprise (SME)	Registered business with some structure and predictable operations.	10–49 employees; audited or semi-audited accounts; formal contracts; access to credit; taxable entity.
Medium Enterprise (SME)	More established business with stable operations and growth potential.	50–249 employees; formal financial statements; HR systems; regular tax filings; higher annual turnover.
Large Enterprise	Fully structured corporate organization.	250+ employees; complex governance; audited annually; multi-departmental structure; high turnover.

How to Think About Your Own Journey: From Informal to Formal

Every entrepreneur begins somewhere, and for most students that starting point is informal, low-risk, and experimental. You test small ideas, earn small amounts, and learn quickly what works and what does not. But if your idea gains momentum, attracts strangers, or shows signs that it could grow beyond your own university, you need a way to think about how and when to take it seriously. The journey from informal hustle to formal business is not a single leap, but a series of conscious steps. The mental model below gives you a simple, practical pathway to follow so you always know where you are in the process, when to formalize, and how to build the foundations of something much bigger than a one-off student gig.

The journey from informal to formal is the journey from student hustler to real entrepreneur (See Table 8 below). Not every idea needs to be formalized, but every student should know *how* and *when* to do it. Informal earns pocket money, formal builds a future. Informal pays rent; formal creates wealth. Informal helps you survive;

formal allows you to scale. I provide below a simple mental model that you can use:

Table 8.	THE JOURNEY FROM INFORMAL TO FORMAL
Step	**What It Means**
1. Start informal	Test ideas cheaply, quickly, and safely before committing time or money.
2. Validate demand	Earn your first £20, £200, then £2,000 to prove real customers genuinely want what you offer.
3. Observe patterns	Notice whether customers return, whether strangers start buying, and whether referrals appear.
4. Assess scalability	Ask whether the idea could work on other campuses or be digitized, automated, or expanded.
5. Formalize when needed	Register a sole proprietorship or LLC once scale, finances, or risk justify becoming a formal entity.
6. Build systems	Develop branding, customer service, basic accounting, marketing, and smooth payment systems.
7. Grow responsibly	Avoid formalizing too early, but never delay once growth, risk or customer expectations demand it.

Most students will never go beyond the informal stage, and there is nothing wrong with that. It simply depends on what kind of student-entrepreneur you want to be. If you want to be a *rich* student – meaning someone who uses their time wisely, avoids waste, builds early wealth, and understands the basic mechanics of business and value creation – then these steps matter. And remember, although I have spent decades working with the World Bank, the British Government, and the European Union as an economist and investor, this is not a technical manual or a hardcore economics textbook. It is a practical guide for students who have been taught almost nothing about money, business, investment, or opportunity, yet are expected to navigate all of it the moment they graduate.

7. Understanding the Nature of Money

Money Isn't for Spending, It's for Building Your Future

If money were a musical instrument, it would be the one instrument capable of playing every sound on the planet. It can take on any role, create any rhythm, and open any stage. The only question is whether you learn how to play it – or spend your life listening to others perform.

You probably go through life believing money is simply something to spend, something you never have enough of, something you wish you had more of, without ever stopping to ask why that is. Most people never challenge themselves to understand the true nature and potential of money. But how could you fly a plane if you had never taken flying lessons? How could you cook exceptional food without dedicating time to mastering the craft? Money is no different. Unless you deliberately learn how it works, what it can become, and how to make it serve you, you will remain its slave for the rest of your life.

They treat every pound, dollar, euro, yuan, rupee or shilling as something that disappears rather than something that can grow. They have never learned that every unit of currency they touch is a tool that can work for them, compound over time, and build freedom if they use it correctly. This chapter gives you a different lens. Money is not just for spending, it is for deploying, multiplying, positioning, and building your future. Until you understand the nature of money beyond consumption, you will always feel like you are running out of it. Once you understand how money really works, you will never see the world the same way again.

Where Does Money Come From?

Most students never stop to think about where money actually comes from. You see it in your account, you earn it from a job, you borrow it as a loan, or you spend it without thinking — but behind the scenes, money is created, distributed, and moved through systems far bigger than your day-to-day life. Understanding where money originates helps you understand why it rises, why it shrinks, why some people build wealth, and why others stay trapped. Once you know how money enters the world, you can start positioning yourself to capture more of it rather than endlessly chasing it.

Most of the money in the world is created not by governments printing notes, but by central banks expanding the money supply and by commercial banks through lending (See Table 9 below) . Under the fractional reserve model, banks are only required to keep a small percentage of deposits on hand — traditionally around 10 percent — and can lend out the rest. This means that for every US$1 actually held in reserve, the banking system can create up to US$10 in new money through loans.

In other words, most of the "money" you see in the world never physically exists; it is created digitally through credit. And the nature of money is changing even further. As the global economy becomes increasingly digital, the future will include central bank digital currencies (CBDCs), alongside the cryptocurrencies and digital assets you already see today. Understanding this shift is essential, because the tools, risks, and opportunities available to you as a student will evolve with it.

Table 9.	YOUR OVERVIEW OF WHERE MONEY COMES FROM
Source of Money	**What It Means**
You earn it	Money you obtain through work, side hustles, freelance tasks, small businesses, or providing value to others.
Governments create it	Central banks print money or expand the money supply digitally through tools like quantitative easing or stimulus.

Table 9. YOUR OVERVIEW OF WHERE MONEY COMES FROM	
Source of Money	**What It Means**
Banks create it	When banks issue loans (student loans, mortgages, credit cards), new money is effectively created in the economy through lending.
Businesses generate it	Companies create money by producing goods and services customers pay for — and pay you for if you work or invest in them.
Investments grow it	Wealth expands through compounding returns: dividends, interest, rising stock prices, real estate appreciation, and rental income.
Markets move it	Inflation, wage changes, prices, and supply chain shifts constantly move money between individuals, businesses, and sectors.
You borrow it	Loans give you temporary access to money you don't yet have, but at the cost of repaying more later through interest.

The True Nature of Money Is Your Biggest Lesson

Money is one of humanity's oldest economic technologies. Archaeological and historical evidence shows that systems of monetary exchange existed thousands of years before modern states or banking institutions emerged. In Mesopotamia, standardized units of account such as the silver shekel were in use nearly 5,000 years ago to price goods, wages, and obligations, even before the widespread circulation of coins (Smithsonian Magazine, 2019).

In ancient China, early forms of money included cowrie shells and metal replicas of shells, used as mediums of exchange as early as the second millennium BCE. These objects functioned as money not because of intrinsic value alone, but because societies collectively accepted them as stores of value and units of account (Smithsonian Magazine, 2019).

Anthropological research further shows that long before coinage, communities across Africa, Asia, and the Middle East used scarce objects such as shells, metals, and livestock as monetary instruments to facilitate trade, settle debts, and signal social trust (Kusimba, 2017). Money, in this sense, predates modern markets. It emerged as a social technology built on trust, shared belief, and collective agreement rather than on paper, coins, or digital code.

Before money, people relied on barter – exchanging one good for another – a system that only works when both sides want exactly what the other has at the same time. Money changed everything. It became a universal medium of exchange, allowing buyers and sellers to trade even if they had nothing the other wanted directly. It became fungible, meaning every unit is interchangeable with another – your dollar is the same as mine, your rupee interchangeable with another rupee. And above all, it became a unit of trust. A banknote, coin, or digital balance has value because society collectively believes it does. Without trust, money collapses.

Over time, money also evolved into a unit of account (a way of measuring value), and a store of value (a way of holding purchasing power for the future). But that last function is where most people misunderstand money. They assume that if they simply hold onto it, their wealth remains intact. In reality, money is a deeply imperfect store of value. Prices rise. Currencies weaken. Governments print more. Optimists call this inflation. Realists call it a slow leak in your financial future.

Artificial intelligence is now reshaping the way money moves, grows, and is understood. AI tools can analyze markets in seconds, forecast trends, scan thousands of data points, and help individuals make far better decisions about budgeting, saving, investing, and managing risk. This does not change the nature of money itself, but it changes your relationship to it, giving you the ability to understand patterns and opportunities that were once visible only to professionals. In a world where financial information moves at extraordinary speed, AI gives you a clearer lens, helping you make smarter choices about how your money is earned, protected and grown.

The very nature of money means that it loses value over time unless you put it to work. Every pound, dollar, euro, yuan, rupee, or shilling you hold is quietly shrinking unless it is invested, deployed, or converted into something that appreciates faster than inflation. Money that sits still decays. Most of you know the pattern already: you might have $3,000 sitting in your account, and then you buy a new iPhone and half of it disappears overnight, even though a phone can be a powerful tool for opportunity. Then you go out for a couple of dinners with friends, and somehow your $3,000 has become $750.

Your rent hits, the bills follow, and before you know it you are staring at $200, panicking, and living under constant financial pressure because everything you have can vanish in a week. When things finally go bad, you end up borrowing, if it's from family, the burden lingers; if it's from the market, the interest rate will destroy you.

Money that is invested grows. Understanding this single truth separates those who remain financially stuck from those who build real independence. Once you understand what money truly is – a tool, a technology, a trust system, and a decaying asset if unused – you begin to grasp why mastering it is essential to your future.

Schools (and often even your parents, as they give you pocket money and don't necessarily teach you how to earn it) never teach you about money beyond spending it. You get money by doing a job. However, because money should be working for you rather than against you, and because you should not spend your life just working for money, understanding the true nature of money is the most fundamental lesson you will ever learn.

Money is without doubt a magical invention. Money enables billions of people to trade, build, invest, cooperate, and grow. You will have heard the sayings 'money does not grow on trees' (unless you are a fruit farmer ;) and "*money makes the world go round.*" These sayings are largely true, not because of the notes or coins themselves, but because of the system of trust, exchange, and possibility they represent.

Table 10 summarizes the true nature of money. Without this understanding, you will spend your entire life playing chess against a Grand Master without ever having learned the value of the pieces, the rules and most opportune moves. Grasping how money works is therefore essential if you ever hope to earn and save money while you sleep — the point at which money finally becomes your servant rather than your master.

Table 10. THE FUNDAMENTAL NATURE OF MONEY		
Concept	**What It Means**	**Why It Matters for You**
Medium of Exchange	Money allows people to trade goods and services without needing a direct swap.	Makes buying and selling easy; you're participating in a massive, efficient system.

Table 10. THE FUNDAMENTAL NATURE OF MONEY		
Concept	What It Means	Why It Matters for You
Unit of Account	Money gives everything a measurable value (prices, wages, rent).	Helps you compare costs, budgets, investments, and financial decisions.
Store of Value	Money holds purchasing power over time – but only imperfectly.	Shows why saving without investing loses value through inflation.
Fungibility	Every unit of money is interchangeable with another of equal value.	Ensures your £10 or ₹100 works exactly like anyone else's – total equality of use.
Divisibility	Money can be divided into smaller units without losing value.	Allows micro-transactions, budgeting, and investing in small amounts.
Durability	Money must withstand physical wear or digital storage without degrading.	Ensures your funds remain usable, whether cash or digital balances.
Portability	Money must be easy to carry or transfer.	Let's you move money instantly (bank apps, mobile money, etc.).
Acceptability	Money is widely accepted in exchange for goods and services.	Your currency is only useful because others trust and accept it.
Uniformity	All units look and behave the same so people trust them.	Prevents fraud and confusion; simplifies transactions.
Limited Supply	Money loses value when too much is created (inflation).	Shows why investing is essential – your cash erodes when supply increases.
Trust-Based Value	Money works because society believes in its value.	Reminds you that money is a belief system – trust makes or breaks it.
Liquidity	Money can be quickly converted into other assets or purchases.	Highlights the flexibility of cash for emergencies and opportunities.
Purchasing Power	The real value of money is what it can buy, not the number printed on it.	Teaches you to focus on *real* wealth, not just nominal balances.
Opportunity Cost	Every pound/dollar spent is one you can't invest or grow.	Helps you prioritize wisely: consumption vs. long-term benefit.
Time Value of Money	Money today is worth more than money tomorrow.	Shows why starting early – even with tiny amounts – is everything.

The Different Kinds of Money

In the modern world, money is no longer just the cash in your pocket. Most of the money you will ever use, earn, lose, or owe will never exist as physical notes. It will be digital, invisible, and flowing through systems you cannot see. Money today includes your bank balance, your loan agreements, your credit lines, your digital payments, your savings, and even the value of assets you own. It includes debt, equity, investments, and financial instruments that behave very differently from cash. Understanding these different forms of money is essential, because each one gives you a different kind of power, risk, or opportunity. The sooner you grasp this; the sooner you can stop being intimidated by money and start using it strategically.

Understanding the True Nature of Debt

Debt is money brought forward from the future, accessed now in exchange for a commitment to repay more later. It becomes a tool or a trap depending on whether it is used to build assets or to fund consumption. Financial theory is clear that debt only adds value when the return it enables exceeds its interest cost (Brealey, Myers and Allen, 2019).

You do not pay income tax on debt, yet you do pay interest, which means debt is only productive when it strengthens your financial position rather than weakens it. When the investment financed by debt produces enough value to cover the principal, pay the interest, and still produces a profit, debt becomes leverage. When it does not, debt becomes a drag that compounds over time and limits your freedom. Wealthy people understand this clearly. They use debt, and often other people's capital, to acquire assets that appreciate faster than the interest rate they pay.

Understanding the True Nature of Equity

Equity represents ownership rather than obligation. When you invest through equity in a company, project, or asset, you are not lending money that must be repaid on fixed terms. You are acquiring a claim on future performance. Your return depends entirely on whether the underlying venture succeeds, grows, or creates value over time.

Unlike debt, equity carries no guaranteed repayment, no fixed interest, and no certainty of outcome. Its value can rise or fall, and in some cases disappear entirely. This makes equity inherently riskier than lending. At the same time, it is precisely this exposure to performance that gives equity its distinctive power. When a business grows, equity holders participate directly in that growth. There is no upper limit on the upside in the way there is with interest-bearing debt.

In financial terms, equity holders sit last in the order of payment. All obligations to lenders must be met before equity receives anything. What remains belongs to the owners. This residual position explains both the risk and the reward of equity. It absorbs losses first, but it also captures gains without a predefined ceiling (Brealey, Myers and Allen, 2019).

For entrepreneurs and companies, equity is a means of raising capital without taking on mandatory repayments that can strain cash flow in early stages. The trade-off is dilution. Issuing equity means sharing ownership, influence, and future gains with others. The decision to use equity is therefore not only financial but strategic. It involves weighing control against growth, independence against scale, and certainty against potential.

For investors, equity is the primary mechanism through which long-term wealth is created. It rewards patience, judgment, and the ability to tolerate uncertainty. Equity does not pay you for time worked. It pays you for ownership held.

Understanding How Debt and Equity Differ

Debt does not dilute ownership, equity does (See Table 11). If you issue equity in a company, you give away a portion of the business, reducing your own share of future profits and control. If instead you finance growth through debt, you retain full ownership but take on an obligation to repay, regardless of whether the business succeeds or fails. Debt is cheaper in terms of control but riskier in terms of cash flow, because repayments are mandatory. Equity is more expensive in terms of control but more flexible in terms of repayment, because investors are paid only if the business performs. Understanding this difference allows you to choose the right instrument for the right purpose, balancing ownership, risk, cash flow, and long-term growth.

Table 11. Debt vs Equity, What They Are and Are Not			
What Debt Is	**What Debt Is Not**	**What Equity Is**	**What Equity Is Not**
A borrowed sum that must be repaid with interest	Free capital with no repayment obligation	Ownership in an asset, business, or project	A guaranteed return or fixed payout
A liability that reduces your net worth until repaid	A creator of wealth by itself	A claim on future profits and asset growth	A loan or a liability owed to others
Leverage that works only if the return exceeds the interest cost	A substitute for savings or discipline	A long-term position that can appreciate over time	Risk-free, liquid, or immune to loss
An external resource used to fund investment or consumption	A permanent source of capital	A share of control, decision-making, or voting rights	A short-term instrument with guaranteed liquidity
A fixed obligation regardless of performance	A flexible cost that adjusts to results	A variable return based on performance	A fixed-income instrument with predetermined payments

The Supply of and Demand for Money

The supply of money in the world is created by trust-based institutions — central banks, commercial banks, and financial systems that expand or contract the amount of money available, as explained earlier. The demand for money, however, is enormous. Countries, companies, and individuals borrow endlessly, which is why the world carries trillions of dollars in debt. Understanding this balance is essential: when money is plentiful, it becomes cheaper to borrow; when it is scarce, it becomes expensive. This is the basic market equilibrium that determines the price of money, better known as interest rates. The same supply-and-demand forces shape exchange rates between currencies — why a dollar, euro, yuan, or shilling rises or falls against another. Entire industries make fortunes trading on these shifts. For you as a student, grasping the simple idea that money, like any other commodity, has a supply, a demand and a price will help you make smarter decisions about borrowing, saving, investing and operating in a global economy.

The Cost of Money, Interest Rates and Inflation

Every time you borrow money – or every time someone lends it to you – there is a cost. That cost is called interest. Interest exists because lending always carries risk, because lenders need to be compensated for giving up access to their money, and because money loses value over time through inflation, meaning tomorrow's money is worth less than today's. One of the biggest differences between a rich student and a poor student is a deep understanding of the nature of money itself — what it costs, why it costs, and how to access it wisely. Whether you are borrowing or lending, you must understand both sides of the equation: the supply side and the demand side. Without this, you will always be at the mercy of money rather than in control of it.

How Does Money Circulate in an Economy?

Every $100 in your pocket is not just sitting still — it is part of a constant flow. The moment you spend it; you pass that $100 to someone else. They then spend it again, perhaps paying a bill, buying food, paying staff, or even paying taxes. That same $100 can touch dozens of hands in a single month. The speed at which money moves from the bank to you, through many other people, and back into the banking system is called the velocity of money. When money circulates quickly, economies feel alive, businesses earn more, wages rise, and opportunity expands. When money slows down, economies feel weak. Central banks measure this through narrow money (cash and easily spendable deposits) and broad money (all the credit, loans and financial assets circulating in the system). Understanding how money moves, how quickly it moves, and how much of it exists tells you a lot about the health of an economy — and how much opportunity is available for you to capture.

Table 12 offers a simple overview of the different forms of money students encounter, how each one works, and why understanding these categories shapes smarter financial decisions. It breaks money down into practical types, showing which kinds help you build wealth, which kinds quietly erode it, and which ones can either accelerate or hinder your future depending on how you use them. This table matters because once you can distinguish between money you spend, money you borrow, money you own, and money that grows while you sleep, you begin to take control of your financial life rather than drifting through it.

Table 12. CATEGORIES OF MONEY STUDENTS MUST UNDERSTAND		
Type of Money	**What It Means**	**Why It Matters for You as a Student**
Cash (Physical or Digital)	The money you see - notes, coins, debit card balance, mobile money.	Useful for daily expenses, but terrible as a long-term store of value because inflation destroys it.
Bank Money	Digital money held in accounts — the majority of modern money.	Easy to use, transfer, and store, but earns little or no interest unless invested.
Credit (Borrowed Money)	Student loans, overdrafts, credit cards — money you *use now* and *repay later*.	Powerful if used strategically (e.g., to build credit), dangerous if misused; high interest will trap you.
Debt Instruments	Mortgages, bonds, personal loans.	Helps you understand how debt funds big purchases and why interest rates can either help or crush you.
Equity (Ownership Money)	Shares in a company, stakes in a business, or ownership of assets.	This is where real wealth grows; equity appreciates and can pay dividends over time.
Savings Money	Money set aside for future use, usually earning low interest.	Safe but slow; good for emergencies, not for long-term wealth building.
Investment Money	Money placed into assets that can grow — stocks, ETFs, real estate, crypto (carefully).	The foundation of creating wealth while you sleep; money works for you instead of you working for it.
Passive Income Money	Money earned without constant effort — dividends, royalties, rental income, business automation.	The goal: income streams that continue even when you stop working.

Table 12. CATEGORIES OF MONEY STUDENTS MUST UNDERSTAND		
Type of Money	**What It Means**	**Why It Matters for You as a Student**
Government-Backed Money (Fiat)	Currency issued by a government, not backed by gold but by trust.	Helps you understand inflation, currency risk, and how governments influence your financial life.
Speculative Money	High-risk, high-reward assets — crypto, early startups, options trading.	Can grow fast or disappear; only for small, calculated risks after you understand the basics.

Interest Rates Affect Borrowing and the Flow of Money

The lower the cost of money (meaning the lower the interest rates), the more people tend to borrow. Cheap borrowing increases spending, investment and business activity, which raises the velocity of money, because money moves faster through the economy. However, when interest rates rise significantly, borrowing becomes expensive. Students borrow less, families borrow less, businesses borrow less. As a result, less money flows through shops, services, salaries and taxes.

The economy slows. This is why the supply and demand for money is always shaped by the price of borrowing: when money is cheap, the economy speeds up; when money is expensive, it slows down. A simple example: if a student loan costs 2 percent interest, many students will take it. If it costs 15 percent interest, far fewer will. The same logic applies to mortgages, credit cards, business loans and even government debt.

Making Money Work for You, Not Against You

For most of you, money is simply a way of getting through the month – paying rent, covering tuition, grabbing food, going pub, and constantly feeling like there is never quite enough. Some students appear "rich" because they inherited money or because their parents can fund their education, but there is another kind of rich student entirely: the one who understands the true nature of money, the power of investment, and the mindset required to turn small amounts into long-term independence.

These students make a conscious decision to treat money not as something to spend, but as one of the most powerful tools ever created for personal freedom. Money buys time, options, security, and choice. But only if you learn how to use it properly. When you understand how to grow it, deploy it and allow it to compound, money becomes an engine that expands your future instead of limiting it. It becomes a lever that lifts you out of the cycle of stress, scarcity and dependence — and into a life shaped by your own decisions rather than by your bank balance.

Table 13 introduces the core principles that determine whether money works for you or slowly works against you. Each idea is simple, practical, and immediately usable for students who want to break out of the cycle of spending, stress, and scarcity. This table matters because mastering these principles early lets you build habits that compound over time, turning small decisions today into major financial advantages later.

Table 13. How to Make Money Work for Not Against You

Principle	What It Means	Why It Matters for You
Spend Less Than You Earn	Your first profit is the gap between income and expenses.	This creates the money you can invest, not just survive on.
Treat Money as a Tool, Not a Toy	Use money to build assets, not just buy things.	Phones, clothes and nights out disappear; assets grow.
Deploy Money, Don't Just Hold It	Money must be invested to beat inflation.	Cash sitting still gets weaker every year.
Build Assets, Not Liabilities	Assets pay you; liabilities drain you.	Choose things that produce income, not bills.
Earn While You Sleep	Build passive income streams – investments, digital products, rentals.	This is the gateway to financial freedom.
Understand the Cost of Borrowing	Interest can make you or break you.	Bad debt traps you; smart debt accelerates you.
Start Early and Let Compounding Work	Small amounts grow massively over time.	The earlier you start, the less you need to invest to get ahead.
Learn How Money Actually Works	Study money the same way you'd study a subject.	It is the most valuable knowledge you'll ever acquire.

Figuring Out Your Relationship to Money

Chapter 2 challenged you to better understand who you are. Chapter 3 posed deep questions to help you identify your true purpose in life and the authentic nature of yourself. These foundations shape everything that follows.

Your relationship with money sits right alongside them. Whether money becomes something you simply earn and spend, or something you learn to use strategically and intentionally to your advantage, is a choice only you can make. The more skills you develop, the more choices you gain. The better your decisions, the better your investments. And the more you learn, practice and apply, the greater the freedoms you will create, for yourself, for your family, and eventually for the world you help shape.

Nature of Money Key Takeaways

Understanding the nature of money is the moment everything in your financial life begins to snap into place. Most people drift through life treating money as something to spend or fear, rather than as a tool to build independence and expand their future. But once you grasp how money is created, how it circulates, how it loses value, and how it can grow, you stop being controlled by money and start controlling what it can do for you. These are the fundamentals that separate the rich student from the poor student, not because one has more money, but because one has more understanding.

- Money loses value over time unless you invest it.

- Money is a tool, not a reward — use it to build assets, not to soothe emotions.

- Inflation silently erodes your savings every year.

- Debt has a cost, and interest is the price of borrowing someone else's money.

- Money moves constantly through the economy — where it moves fastest, opportunity grows.

- Most money isn't physical; it's digital, created through trust and lending.

- Wealth comes from understanding money, not from chasing more of it.

- If you don't learn how money works, you'll spend your life working for someone who has.

8. IDENTIFYING OPPORTUNITY

Learning to Live an Abundance Mindset

At the beginning of this book, we explored the two mindsets that shape every financial future: scarcity and abundance. A scarcity mindset sees limits; an abundance mindset sees possibilities. But abundance is not about blind optimism or wishful thinking. Developing an abundance mindset means learning to see the true nature of the world you are about to transact in. It means recognizing patterns, noticing gaps, understanding needs, and observing the places where things break, slow down, or frustrate people. Above all, it means seeing opportunities that most people overlook.

Learning to Develop an Abundance Mindset

Your greatest advantage as a student entrepreneur is simple: you can learn to see what others do not. This is perhaps the greatest lesson you can ever learn, even if the education system does not teach it to you. This book does. Opportunities hide in gaps, gaps in markets, services, people's needs, convenience, price, speed, quality, friction, and in the everyday frustrations that everyone experiences but almost no one studies. Every business in the world exists because someone noticed a gap and stepped forward to fill it.

Artificial intelligence strengthens this ability to notice what others miss. With simple prompts you can scan thousands of reviews, spot patterns in complaints, test demand across markets, or compare dozens of existing solutions in seconds. AI does not replace the instinct to observe, it accelerates it, helping you recognize genuine gaps faster and with far greater clarity. It gives you a wider lens, allowing you to validate whether the problem you see locally also exists nationally or globally, and whether a simple student idea might have far larger potential.

But identifying opportunity requires more than noticing annoyance or inconvenience. It demands active participation. When something goes wrong, or when you feel a moment of friction, do not just complain or shrug. Interrogate it. Ask yourself: Do other people have this problem too? How many? What would a simple solution look like? Could I design it? Could I be the solution? This is the shift from being a passive consumer of experiences to becoming an active creator of solutions.

Opportunities rarely arrive fully formed. They show up as irritations, inefficiencies, delays, confusion, or unmet desires. Most people simply tolerate those moments and move on. The student entrepreneur stops, pays attention, and steps into the space where value can be created. This chapter will teach you how to tune your senses to these gaps and turn them into the beginnings of real businesses, ideas that start small but can grow into powerful engines of income, freedom, and independence.

How Abundance Thinkers See the World

Abundance thinkers have a habit that sets them apart from almost everyone else. They pay attention. They observe carefully. They notice what others overlook and ask questions others never think to ask. Many of the greatest inventions in human history were created because someone saw a small problem, a tiny irregularity, or a moment of frustration and refused to walk past it. They did not accept the world as it was. They imagined how it could be.

ABUNDANCE MINDSET

Here are some powerful examples that show how abundance thinkers have changed history simply by seeing differently:

- **The intermittent windscreen wiper**: Robert Kearns noticed that the human eye blinks intermittently, not continuously. Years later, stuck in light rain, he realized car wipers should work the same way. A single observation about blinking turned into a global automotive standard.

- **The paper clip**: The humble paper clip is one of the most successful inventions in history. It solved a tiny but universal problem, keeping papers together without pins, glue, or string. Its inventor saw people fumbling with pages and imagined a small piece of bent wire that could grip without damaging. It was simple, cheap, elegant, and absolutely transformative.

- **Velcro**: Swiss engineer George de Mestral took a walk with his dog and noticed burrs sticking to its fur. Instead of ignoring them, he examined the burrs under a microscope and discovered their hook-like structure. This led to Velcro, used in clothing, shoes, equipment, and aerospace.

- **Post-it Notes**: Post-it Notes were invented by accident. A scientist at 3M created a weak adhesive that did not seem useful. Another colleague realized it could be used on paper for notes that stick lightly without damage. A failed glue became a global stationery essential.

- **The Snapchat idea**: Evan Spiegel and his classmates wanted messages that could disappear, because not everything should stay online forever. They noticed a small social problem and built a simple solution. It became Snapchat, used by hundreds of millions.

- **The first version of Facebook**: Mark Zuckerberg created a basic campus directory because students wanted to connect and share information more easily. He solved a simple community need and used universities as a test bed. The idea scaled into one of the largest platforms in history.

- **Solving accommodation problems**: Students struggle every term with room changes, move-ins, storage, transport, and finding affordable furniture. An abundance thinker asks: what is the simplest solution to reduce stress, cost, and time? Examples include storage services, furniture exchanges, or short-term sublets managed through a simple matching platform.

- **Helping with academic or research challenges**: Students waste countless hours searching for reliable summaries, research materials, or peer feedback. An abundance thinker sees this as an opportunity to create curated study guides, research support services, or peer matching systems that help students finish work faster.

Abundance thinkers are not geniuses. They are observers. They pay attention to the world around them and listen to problems instead of ignoring them. They understand that frustration is a clue, inefficiency is a signal, and every small inconvenience could be the beginning of a new idea. That mindset is what separates those who wait for opportunity from those who create it.

Noticing What Others Ignore

Noticing opportunity is not always about inventing something new. Often it is about *reinventing* something that already exists or simply *copying* a good idea from another place and adapting it to your own environment. If a student in another country has created a clever solution for accommodation, transport, study support, or daily convenience, you can often replicate the model, provided it is not patented or legally protected. Many of the most successful businesses in history were not original ideas, just better versions of old ones applied in new ways.

The real skill is not originality. The real skill is learning to observe reality differently. Most people drift through life consuming, spending, and reacting. An abundance thinker pauses, notices, and asks questions. Why is this happening? Why does this problem still exist? Why does nobody fix it? What would happen if I did not ignore it? What could it become?

To build this habit, carry a small notebook with you, a simple abundance book. Every time you see a gap, frustration, inconvenience, or pattern, write it down. At the end of the week, review your notes and look for signals. Over time you will train your mind to see what others walk past, and those observations will become the raw material for ideas that may shape your future.

Turning Problems into Opportunities

Albert Einstein once remarked to '*Stay away from negative people. They have a problem for every solution.*' (Bartlett's Familiar Quotations, n.d.). Abundance thinkers reverse this. They see a solution hiding inside every problem. Where others complain, they investigate. Where others accept difficulty, they look for a better way. Where others see an obstacle, they see raw material for a new idea. The world is full of problems, but only a small number of people ever stop long enough to ask what those problems are worth.

When you learn to treat every friction, delay, inconvenience, or frustration as a signal, the world begins to reveal opportunities everywhere. You shift from reacting to problems to mining them for value. The key is to train yourself to look beyond the irritation and ask: *Who else has this problem? How often does it happen? What would life look like if it disappeared? And could I be the one to remove it? How much would the solution to generate?*

Table 14 below provides some basic guidance to you on how to turn everyday problems into practical opportunities.

Table 14. HOW TO TURN PROBLEMS INTO OPPORTUNITIES				
Common Problem	**Underlying Need**	**Opportunity Question**	**Possible Solution**	**Why It Works**
People waste time waiting or queuing	Speed and convenience	How can this be faster or more predictable?	Booking systems, automation, pre-order services	Saves time and reduces stress
People struggle to find what they need	Access and clarity	How can I make it easier to locate, compare, or choose?	Search tools, guides, curated bundles	Reduces decision fatigue
People repeat tasks they dislike	Ease and efficiency	Can someone do this for them, or simplify the task?	Outsourcing, done-for-you services, templates	Removes frustration
People pay too much for basic things	Affordability and fairness	Can I provide the same value at a lower cost?	Low-cost alternatives, repurposed goods	Helps budget-conscious users
People get stuck or confused	Guidance and reassurance	What would help them feel more confident or informed?	Tutorials, mentoring, information tools	Enhances confidence and completion

Spotting Gaps in Markets and Needs

One of the most important skills you can develop as a student entrepreneur is the ability to recognize gaps in what people want, what people need, and what people are willing to pay for. These gaps exist everywhere. In fact, most markets are full of them, but only a few people ever notice. When you learn to observe carefully, listen closely, and question what others accept, you begin to see where value is missing and where new opportunities can take shape.

Gaps appear when something is too slow, too expensive, too complicated, too inconvenient, too limited, or simply not good enough. They also appear when people desire something that is unavailable or poorly delivered. Spotting these gaps is your advantage. Once you train your mind to identify them, you can understand why existing solutions fall short and how a better, faster, or cheaper version could find an audience. This is the foundation of entrepreneurial thinking.

Table 15 shows why every frustration, delay, or overpriced product in your daily life is actually a hidden opportunity. By breaking down the different types of gaps that exist in markets, it trains you to recognize where value is missing and where simple fixes can create new income ideas. This matters for students because once you learn to spot these gaps, you can turn everyday problems into practical business opportunities that others routinely overlook.

Table 15. TYPES OF GAPS IN MARKETS AND WHAT THEY REVEAL			
Type of Gap	**What It Means**	**Questions to Ask**	**Example of Opportunity**
Value Gap	Current options cost too much for what they offer	Can I provide the same value at a lower price?	Affordable versions of overpriced essentials
Convenience Gap	Something is hard to access or takes too long	How can I make this easier or faster?	Delivery, pickup, or booking services
Quality Gap	Existing solutions are unreliable or poor quality	What would a higher quality version look like?	Better-made or curated products
Access Gap	People cannot reach or find what they need	Can I bring the solution closer to them?	Localized services or digital discovery tools
Experience Gap	People dislike the process of using a product or service	How can I make the experience smoother?	Simplified processes, guides, or redesigns

Rich Student. Poor Student.

Type of Gap	What It Means	Questions to Ask	Example of Opportunity
Knowledge Gap	People want something but lack information	Can I help them understand or choose better?	Tutorials, summaries, comparison tools

Table 15. TYPES OF GAPS IN MARKETS AND WHAT THEY REVEAL

When you learn to spot gaps in markets and needs, you stop accepting the world as it is and begin imagining how it could be improved. This connects directly to the earlier chapters. Once you recognize a genuine opportunity, you no longer see the money you have as something to spend. You begin to see it as something to commit toward solving a problem with a high potential return. Money becomes a tool for investing in ideas, testing solutions, and creating value rather than something that disappears through consumption. When you think this way, you shift from spending what you have to building what you need, and you move closer to becoming the kind of student who grows wealth instead of watching it vanish.

Seeing Friction as a Business Signal

Friction is one of the clearest indicators that opportunity is nearby. Whenever something feels slow, confusing, frustrating, expensive, inconvenient, or unnecessarily complicated, it is a signal that value is missing. Most people simply tolerate these moments and move on, but abundance thinkers pay attention. Friction reveals where people waste time, lose money, feel stressed, or face barriers. If you learn to observe these moments rather than ignore them, you begin to see where a better process, product, or service could exist.

A powerful global example is the rise of digital currencies and cryptocurrencies. Traditional money transfers often involve delays, paperwork, fees, and layers of intermediaries. Moving money internationally can take days and cost a significant percentage of the amount transferred. Digital currencies challenged this friction entirely by making the exchange of value almost instantaneous and paperless. These systems reduce costs, remove bureaucratic barriers, save time, and reduce the environmental impact associated with paper-based transactions. They exist because innovators recognized the friction in traditional finance and imagined a frictionless alternative.

In many cases, the simplest businesses are built by removing a small piece of friction that thousands of people experience every day. Types of friction are summarized in Table 16 below.

Table 16. COMMON TYPES OF FRICTION AND WHAT THEY REVEAL

Type of Friction	What It Tells You	Opportunity Question	Possible Direction
Slow processes	Time is being wasted	How can this be faster?	Automation, pre-ordering, queue reduction
Confusing systems	People feel stuck or unsure	How can this be clearer or simpler?	Tutorials, redesigns, step-by-step tools
High costs	Current options are overpriced	How can this be more affordable?	Lower-cost alternatives or bundles
Limited access	People cannot get what they need when they need it	How can I bring it closer?	Delivery, on-demand access, localized solutions
Repetitive tasks	People dislike doing the same thing repeatedly	How can this be done for them?	Outsourcing, service models, templates
Poor quality	People feel dissatisfied	What would a better version look like?	Higher-quality or curated products

Asking the Right Questions

There are countless ways to think about problems and solutions, but the students who excel are the ones who learn to ask better questions than everyone around them. Abundance is everywhere. Every song ever written is unique, yet all are made from the same few musical notes. Every book in history is different, yet all are built from the same alphabet. Opportunity works the same way. The raw materials are everywhere. Your advantage comes from the quality of the questions you ask when you face a situation that others barely notice.

Asking better questions forces you to see beyond the surface. It trains you to use the tools you have learned in this book to examine problems from multiple angles. The right questions reveal gaps, clarify needs, illuminate risks, and point toward solutions. They transform ordinary observations into the beginnings of new ideas and, in time, real businesses. Questions turn confusion into clarity, friction into opportunity, and uncertainty into strategy.

Table 17 gives you a practical set of questions that turn ordinary problems into real business opportunities. Each category shows you how to think more deeply about what you observe, how to design smarter solutions, and how to judge whether an idea is worth your time. This matters for students because good questions lead to better decisions. When you learn to analyze problems with this kind of structure, you stop guessing and start evaluating ideas the same way successful entrepreneurs do, making it far easier to pick the opportunities that can actually work.

Table 17.	KEY QUESTIONS THAT TURN PROBLEMS INTO OPPORTUNITIES	
Category	Questions to Ask	Why It Matters
Understanding the Problem	What exactly is happening here? Why does this problem exist? Who else experiences it?	Helps you identify the real need rather than the surface symptom.
Designing a Solution	How could this be done differently? Is there a simpler or faster way? What would the ideal solution look like?	Encourages creativity and reveals whether a better alternative is possible.
Evaluating the Business Potential	Can this become a business? How big could the market be? How often does the problem occur?	Helps you assess whether the idea is commercially viable.
Assessing Scalability	Could this work in other places? Could it be automated or digitized? Can it grow beyond me?	Shows whether the opportunity has long-term potential.
Building the Right Team	What skills do I lack? Who could I partner with? Who has strengths that complement mine?	Reminds you that you do not have to do everything alone.
Financing and Resources	What would it cost to start? Who might finance this? What resources do I already have?	Helps you think about feasibility without being discouraged by cost.
Strategic Positioning	Who are the competitors? What makes my solution different? Where is the gap that others have missed?	Teaches you how to stand out and avoid crowded spaces.

Peter J. Middlebrook

How to Observe Like an Entrepreneur

Observing like an entrepreneur is not just about noticing problems. It is about deciding which problems are worth your time and which ones are not. Once you identify a potential gap or friction point, you need a simple internal checklist to evaluate whether the idea has real potential or whether it should be discarded. Entrepreneurs do not chase every idea they encounter. They observe carefully, then analyze quickly. Their goal is to understand whether a problem can become a viable business, how large that business might become, and whether the effort and risk involved are justified.

Entrepreneurs look at a problem and immediately begin evaluating it in practical terms. Could this idea earn one hundred dollars a month, or could it earn one thousand? Is this a tiny opportunity or something that could scale to other campuses, cities, or countries? What skills do I lack that someone else could provide? How much time or money would I need to invest? What are the risks, and what would failure cost me? What would success look like, and who would benefit? This quiet evaluation is the difference between idle daydreaming and meaningful opportunity recognition.

While this book explores every level of opportunity, from small side incomes to larger scalable ventures, most of you will simply be looking for ways to earn an extra two, three, four or five hundred dollars a month. Some of the ideas you discover will stay small and practical, others may grow into something far greater. As most of you will be risk averse, since the capital you have must be protected to pay for your education, this checklist helps you decide whether an income earning opportunity you have identified is likely to turn a profit.

Table 18 gives you a clear, step-by-step way to judge whether an idea is worth pursuing before you spend time, money, or energy on it. Each stage shows you how experienced entrepreneurs think, moving from understanding the problem to assessing risk and strategic fit. This matters for students because it prevents wasted effort and helps you focus only on ideas that have real demand, realistic execution, and long-term potential, rather than chasing every opportunity that appears.

Table 18.	THE ENTREPRENEUR'S OPPORTUNITY EVALUATION CHECKLIST	
Evaluation Step	**Key Questions Entrepreneurs Ask**	**Why It Matters**
Validate the Problem	Is this a real problem for many people, or just an inconvenience for me? How often does it occur?	Ensures you focus on problems with real demand, not personal annoyances.
Estimate Earning Potential	Could this idea earn fifty to one hundred dollars a month, or could it earn five hundred to one thousand? Could it scale beyond that?	Helps you understand whether the idea is worth the time invested.
Assess Scalability	Could this work on multiple campuses, or in other cities or countries? Can it be automated or standardized?	Determines long-term potential rather than short-term pocket money.
Evaluate Resources Needed	How much money, time, or skill will this require? Do I have these resources, or do I need partners?	Prevents you from pursuing ideas you cannot realistically execute alone.
Identify Partners and Skills	What skills do I lack? Who could join me to build this? What strengths do others bring that I do not?	Encourages collaboration and reduces personal risk.
Analyze Risks	What is the downside? What happens if this fails? What is the cost of failure?	Allows you to choose low-risk, high-upside ideas first.
Consider Strategic Fit	Does this idea align with who I am, what I am good at, and where I want to go?	Ensures the idea fits your identity and long-term goals.

Deciding When to Invest

Once you have identified a potential opportunity and evaluated it with the checklist, the next question is simple: should you invest your time, your money, or neither. Most student entrepreneurs fail not because they choose the wrong ideas, but because they commit too much too early, or too little too late. Deciding when to invest is both an art and a discipline.

Invest only when three things are clear. First, that the problem is real for a significant number of people. Second, that the cost of testing your idea is low enough that failure does not harm your ability to pay for your education or living costs. Third, that the potential reward, even at a small scale, justifies the energy required. If an idea can earn you fifty, one hundred or even five hundred dollars a month safely and consistently, it may be worth exploring. If the idea requires heavy spending, specialized equipment or complicated legal steps at the start, walk away for now. The goal at this stage is not to make a fortune, but to find safe, smart and realistic opportunities that build your confidence and capability over time.

Testing Your Idea

Entrepreneurs learn by doing. The safest way to move forward is to test a very small version of your idea before committing fully. This is how you train your intuition, build judgment, and reduce risk. A test should be quick, simple and inexpensive. You might speak to ten students to ask whether they would pay for your solution. You might create a basic version of your service and offer it to a small group. You might sketch a product concept and gather feedback. These micro experiments teach you more than months of thinking ever will.

The key is to design tests that are fast and reversible. You should never risk your tuition money, your rent or your essential savings. Small experiments allow you to watch how people respond, to refine your idea, and to learn whether the opportunity is worth pursuing. Testing builds confidence and capacity, and training your entrepreneurial instincts through repeated practice strengthens your ability to evaluate bigger ideas later in life.

Training Your Mind Daily

Entrepreneurial thinking grows through habit, not occasional inspiration. To train your mind daily, carry a small notebook or keep a notes app open. Record problems you see, patterns you notice, and frustrations you hear. Review your notes at the end of each week and look for repeated themes.

This simple practice strengthens your ability to observe, filter and connect ideas. Over time, you will start noticing opportunities automatically. You will think differently, ask sharper questions and see possibilities where others see nothing. This daily training is how you build the mindset of a creator rather than a consumer, and it becomes one of the most powerful skills you carry into the rest of your life.

Identifying Opportunity – Key Takeaways

Rich Student. Poor Student.

Identifying opportunity is a skill that grows with attention, curiosity, and practice. It is the shift from drifting through the world as a consumer to moving through it as a creator. Once you learn how to see patterns, gaps, friction, and value, you stop waiting for permission and start shaping possibilities. These takeaways are your shortcut to thinking like an entrepreneur, using what you see to build income, confidence and independence while still a student.

- Opportunity hides in gaps, frustrations, needs, delays and inefficiencies.

- Every complaint you hear from others is data that can be turned into value.

- Not every idea is worth pursuing; evaluate it with simple filters before investing time or money.

- Start small. Test simple versions of your idea to learn quickly and safely.

- Think in terms of value, not effort. The best ideas remove friction or create convenience.

- You do not need to invent something original. Copy, adapt or improve what already works.

- Small ideas can earn you fifty, one hundred or five hundred dollars a month. This matters.

- Your mind improves through daily practice. Observe closely, question constantly, and note everything.

- When you find a real opportunity, treat money as a tool, not something to spend.

- The habit of seeing opportunity is what separates those who wait for life from those who build it.

Later in the book, Chapter 11 expands this mindset into practice by giving you a wide set of real examples, ideas, and starting points. Think of it as a catalogue of possibilities to activate your abundance mentality as you design your own path."

9. CHOOSING YOUR INCOME STRATEGY

Build Your Income Future Now - Starting from Where You Are

Choosing the right income strategy is not always obvious. Just because you have a particular talent does not mean that talent is what the market is looking for or what will serve you best. You may be an exceptional guitarist, but giving guitar lessons can only ever reach a limited ceiling of income, no matter how brilliant you are. Many students enjoy photography, but in a digital and AI-driven world, photography has shifted from a high-value craft to a crowded and declining profession. Coding is another example. Five years ago it was promoted as the essential career skill. Today, large parts of coding can be produced instantly by AI tools. A skill you possess is not always the skill the market rewards, and it may not be the best use of your time, your energy or your ambitions.

What matters is not only alignment but income viability. The income strategy you choose must fit who you are, what you want and how you want your future to look, but it must also give you a realistic path to generating profit in a world where markets, technology and expectations are shifting rapidly. It is important to differentiate between working and earning. You can dig a hole in the sand for twelve hours a day and then fill it in again and you will be extremely busy and extremely fit, but you will not earn a single cent. Activity is not the same as income. You need to identify actions that turn a profit, build momentum, lay the foundations for financial independence, and over time move you towards being self-employed, a business owner, or an investor with passive income or multiple passive income streams, even if you continue to earn income elsewhere.

This section guides you through how to select an income strategy that matches your skills, your purpose and your financial goals. The next chapter provides a full buffet of practical options; a myriad of ideas designed to energize your thinking and help you choose strategies that can thrive in the market you have access to.

You All Have a Different Starting Point

Every one of you begins from a different starting point and recognizing that truth is essential before choosing any income strategy. Some of you grew up with comfort, stability and parental support. Others have navigated pressure, uncertainty and responsibility since childhood. Some of you have parents funding your education, accommodation and food, allowing you to focus fully on your studies. Others are juggling part-time jobs, late-night shifts and weekend work just to stay afloat. Some of you were born into wealth, others into poverty. Some live in major global cities where money and opportunity move fast. Others live in rural areas in Africa, Asia or small towns where life is slower and pathways less obvious. Every starting point matters because it shapes the world you see around you.

Some of you arrive at university with strong networks, mentors, alumni contacts or family connections. Others arrive completely alone. Some of you have access to equipment, land, buildings or capital. Some of you are sharing a small, rented room with several other people, working shifts at McDonald's to cover basic living costs. Some of you are brilliant at technology. Others are not. Some of you study business or engineering. Some of you study art, poetry or music. Some of you come from homes where financial literacy was normal. Others come from homes where money was a source of stress or silence. None of these things define your future, but they do define your present reality.

You also come from different identities and life experiences. You are male, female or transgender. You come from different ethnic backgrounds. You live on different continents, in different countries, speaking different languages, operating in different markets. Some of you live in environments that are business-friendly, open and flexible like the United States. Others live in systems controlled by small elite groups where access to capital or opportunity is harder to find. These differences matter because they shape your personal investment strategy.

The advantage you have today is that the world around you is changing faster than at any other point in human history. Most of you now have access to the internet, meaning you can plug into global markets regardless of where you live. You can sell services, products, ideas and skills to anyone on the planet. Geography no longer sets your ceiling. AI has also democratized knowledge, making skills, tools and information available to almost everyone. The world is not perfectly fair, but it is far more level than it has ever been.

Whatever your starting point is, that is your starting point. You cannot change it, but you can change everything that comes after it. Your task is to choose the income strategy that fits your reality today, while visualizing the life you want two, three, five or ten years from now. You need to understand your starting point, and project out, before working towards the persons you want to see. This book is designed to help you bridge that gap. Table 19 helps you to better understand your own personal starting point.

Table 19. STARTING POINT CHECKLIST FOR STUDENTS		
Category	Questions You Need to Answer	What You Should Write Down
Personal Skills	What skills do you already have? What do people say you are good at? What comes naturally to you?	Technical skills, creative skills, communication ability, academic strengths, problem solving ability, languages, digital skills.
Personal Interests	What activities energize you? What topics keep your attention? What do you enjoy learning or doing?	Subjects you love, hobbies, passions, areas you can talk about for hours.
Education and Knowledge	What are you studying? What knowledge do you already have that others might value?	Your major, your courses, your specialist knowledge, tools you can use because of your studies.

Rich Student. Poor Student.

Table 19. STARTING POINT CHECKLIST FOR STUDENTS

Category	Questions You Need to Answer	What You Should Write Down
Networks and Relationships	Who do you know? Who can you ask for advice or support? Who believes in you?	Friends, classmates, teachers, mentors, family contacts, alumni links, online communities.
Financial Situation	How much money do you have access to right now? Do you earn income? Do you have savings? Do you have debts?	Savings, part time income, grants, scholarships, family support, debts, financial constraints.
Physical Resources and Assets	What do you own or have access to that others find useful?	Phone, laptop, internet access, transportation, tools, equipment, extra space, land, buildings, campus facilities.
Environment and Location	Where do you live and study? What opportunities come with that environment?	Big city, small town, rural area, developing country, developed country, on campus, off campus.
Market Opportunities Around You	Who are the people near you? What do they need? What do they complain about?	Student needs, campus gaps, local business gaps, community problems, regional shortages.
Digital and Online Opportunities	What online platforms can you access? What can you sell or create digitally?	Freelancing sites, e commerce, digital content, global clients, remote services.
Strengths and Advantages	What do you have that others your age do not?	Unique knowledge, languages, location advantages, access to networks, personality traits.
Constraints and Limitations	What holds you back right now? What challenges do you need to work around?	Time limits, financial pressure, weak internet, lack of networks, difficult family situation.
Personal Identity and Context	What aspects of your background shape your opportunities?	Gender, ethnicity, language, culture, country, local market conditions, political or economic constraints.
Technology and AI Capability	How well can you use technology? Can you leverage AI tools to boost your productivity?	Digital skills, AI tools you know, willingness to learn, access to software.

Table 19. STARTING POINT CHECKLIST FOR STUDENTS		
Category	**Questions You Need to Answer**	**What You Should Write Down**
Long Term Vision	Where do you want to be in two years? Five years? Ten years?	Your desired location, lifestyle, career direction, income goals, life purpose.
Immediate Starting Position	Based on all the above, where exactly are you today?	A summary statement of who you are, what you have and what you can use right now to begin.

Identify Your Primary Advantages

Once you understand your starting point, your next step is to identify the various advantages you already possess. Every one of you carries a mix of strengths, constraints and hidden resources that can shape the income strategy you choose. These advantages fall into three categories. A competitive advantage is something you do better than most people around you. A comparative advantage is something you can do with less effort, cost or difficulty than others. A collaborative advantage is the value you create when you combine your skills, networks or resources with someone else. Learning to recognize these will help you position yourself correctly in the market you are entering.

ADVANTAGES

DISADVANTAGES

COMPETETIVE

UNCOMPETETIVE

NO COMPARATIVE
ADVANTAGES

COMPARATIVE

SUCCESS

COLLABORATIVE

UNCOLLABORATIVE

Competitive Advantages

A competitive advantage is the edge you create through skill, speed, knowledge, or discipline that lets you outperform others in the same activity. For example, in growing my business, I worked 100 to 120-hour weeks, 365 days of the year, and did not take a holiday for the first eight years, not even a day. That level of commitment is a competitive advantage I have. If someone works 9 to 5, Monday to Friday, that is a valid choice, but they will not be able to beat me in areas where I am committing far more time and intensity.

A student with a competitive advantage could potentially study more efficiently, solve problems faster, or produce higher quality work than peers in the same subject or task. If you develop strong coding skills while others are still learning the basics, you can take on paid freelancing projects or build apps that generate income while they are still catching up. Competitive advantages are built, not given.

Comparative Advantages

A comparative advantage is the edge you already have because of your natural strengths, background, location, or circumstances, even if you are not the absolute best. It is about relative efficiency rather than total dominance. For example, if you live next to a textile industry, you have easier access to suppliers, knowledge, and opportunities that make it more efficient for you to engage in textiles. If you live near Wall Street, and particularly if you are a US citizen with access to those networks and institutions, you have a natural advantage in learning about finance, seeking internships, or entering that sector.

If your country grows bananas and has the right land, climate, and export networks, then producing and exporting bananas becomes a comparative advantage. Countries without fertile land for bananas simply cannot match that efficiency. These differences matter for students too. You might not be the top designer in the world, but if you can produce work faster or more easily than your classmates, it is sensible to focus your time there. Comparative advantage helps you choose activities where your starting position gives you the greatest return.

Collaborative Advantages

A collaborative advantage is the strength you gain when working with others in ways that expand what you can achieve on your own. Some people are highly gregarious and thrive in teams, while others prefer to work independently. Collaboration is not always an advantage, and many individuals succeed as solo operators with full control over their pace, decisions, and output.

Still, when collaboration works well, it unlocks positive multipliers that extend far beyond your personal limits. You gain access to skill sets you do not have, viewpoints you might never consider, and capabilities that broaden the scale or speed of what you can build. For example, you might pair your design skills with a friend who codes and another who understands marketing, allowing the group to create a product none could build alone. A collaborative advantage is not universal, but for those who can use it, the combined strengths of a team can move you further and faster than individual effort alone.

Table 20 helps you understand the different types of advantages you already carry and how each one shapes the income strategies that suit you best. By breaking your strengths into competitive, comparative, and collaborative categories, it shows you where you naturally excel, where you have built an edge through effort, and where teamwork can multiply your results. This matters for students because the fastest way to earn more is to choose opportunities that align with the strengths you already possess, rather than forcing yourself into work that fights against your nature.

Table 20. PERSONAL ADVANTAGE ASSESSMENT MATRIX				
Category	**For You**	**Advantages**	**Disadvantages**	**Income Impact**
Competitive Advantage Strengths you build through effort, discipline, skill, or intensity.	What do I do better, faster, or more consistently than others because I put in more work or have stronger skills?	Working longer hours, mastering coding early, producing high quality content quickly, top exam technique, strong discipline.	Low discipline, inconsistent output, slower learning pace, weak time management.	Highly competitive advantages point you toward fields where performance and speed matter, such as freelancing, trading, consulting, tutoring, or any skill-based work.
Comparative Advantage Strengths based on natural background, location, or circumstances that make you relatively more efficient in certain tasks.	What comes easily to me compared to others? What resources or circumstances do I have access to that others do not?	Living near a textile industry, living near Wall Street, growing up in a business family, bilingual skills, access to equipment or networks, living in a banana producing country.	Lack of local industry support, limited networks, weak natural aptitude in a topic, no access to relevant tools or environment.	Strong comparative advantages suggest choosing income streams where your existing position gives you a head start, such as design, sales, language tutoring, industry-based work, or sector specific micro businesses.
Collaborative Advantage	Do I work well in teams,	Being highly gregarious,	Difficulty collaborating,	Strong collaborative

85

Table 20. PERSONAL ADVANTAGE ASSESSMENT MATRIX

Category	For You	Advantages	Disadvantages	Income Impact
Strengths unlocked by working with others, combining talent and viewpoints to achieve more than you could alone.	manage groups, or build partnerships easily? Or do I prefer independent work?	forming strong teams, knowing how to divide tasks, having friends with complementary skills.	preference for solo work, conflict in teams, lack of trust in group settings.	advantages align well with group projects, start-up teams, joint ventures, co built digital products, and shared income projects. Weak collaborative advantages point toward solo paths such as writing, trading, coding, tutoring, or independent content creation.

Understanding Different Categories of Income

Before you choose an income strategy that fits your life, you need to understand the different types of income available to you. Not all income is created equal. Some forms require constant effort, some scale beautifully, and some can be built while you study, while others will only take shape later in life. When you understand the categories clearly, you stop confusing movement with progress. You know exactly what kind of income you are building, what it demands and what it can become.

Every one of you will eventually build your wealth from a mix of different income streams, but the order in which you build them depends on your starting point, your skills, your risk appetite and the competitive, comparative and collaborative advantages you identified earlier. The table below summarizes the primary paths to wealth that you should focus on first, together with the secondary streams that many students overlook but are crucial for long-term wealth building.

What these different income categories mean for you is simple, but powerful.

Right now, your income might come from whatever you can do nearby, such as laboring around the corner, tutoring, serving food, or taking on gig work. That is earned income, and when you stop working, the money stops. Many of you might prefer a different path, such as building a small business that eventually produces passive or semi passive income. Every business owner begins by doing everything themselves, whether that is running a café, selling products, or building a service.

In the early stages, you are the one behind the counter, the designer, the marketer, and the manager. Only when the business grows can you hire others and move into oversight, where income continues even when you are not physically present. The table below helps you understand where your current income sits, what you might want to move towards, and which steps will take you from where you are today to the income mix you want to build over time.

Table 21 gives you a clear overview of the different types of income you can build as a student, how difficult each one is, and what kind of long-term wealth it can realistically create. It shows the practical differences between income you earn by working, income you build through a business, and income that grows even when you stop. This matters for students because choosing the right income path early can dramatically change your financial future, helping you avoid dead-end effort and focus instead on strategies that compound, scale, and strengthen your long-term independence.

Table 21. THE BASIC CATEGORIES OF INCOME					
Category of Income	**Aligns To (Primary/Secondary Path)**	**What It Means**	**Examples Students Can Build**	**Effort Required**	**Long-Term Wealth Potential**
Active Income	**Earned Income (Primary)**	You trade time for money. Money stops when you stop working.	Tutoring, part-time jobs, freelancing, gig work, campus services.	High and ongoing.	Low unless transitioned into something scalable.
Service-Based Entrepreneurial Income	**Earned Income → Business Income (Secondary)**	You offer services you control, set the price for, and can	Video editing, design services, social media managem	Medium to high at the start; reduces once systemized.	Medium. Can grow into a small business.

Table 21.	THE BASIC CATEGORIES OF INCOME				
Category of Income	Aligns To (Primary/Secondary Path)	What It Means	Examples Students Can Build	Effort Required	Long-Term Wealth Potential
		eventually outsource or scale.	ent, consulting.		
Product-Based Income	Passive Income (Primary)	You create something once and sell it repeatedly without trading extra hours.	Digital downloads, e-books, templates, online courses, merchandise.	High at creation; low when selling.	High. Scales endlessly without extra time.
Platform or Audience Income	Passive Income (Primary)	You monetize attention rather than labor. Income grows with the size of your audience.	YouTube, podcasts, TikTok, blogs with ads, affiliate revenue.	High early investment; slow ramp-up.	Very high once established.
Commission or Performance-Based Income	Earned Income + Passive Hybrid (Primary)	You earn based on sales or outcomes, giving leverage beyond your direct hours.	Affiliate marketing, sales commissions, referral fees.	Medium; Requires outreach and consistency.	Medium to high depending on scale.
Business Ownership Income	Business Income (Secondary)	Income from systems, teams or infrastructure you build. The business	Student-run agencies, online stores with automation,	High early investment; reduces over time.	Very high. Core of long-term wealth.

Rich Student. Poor Student.

Table 21.	THE BASIC CATEGORIES OF INCOME				
Category of Income	Aligns To (Primary/Secondary Path)	What It Means	Examples Students Can Build	Effort Required	Long-Term Wealth Potential
		earns even when you are not present.	subscription services.		
Passive Investment Income	Portfolio Income + Passive Income (Primary)	Income from money working for you instead of you working for money.	Dividends, ETFs, interest, capital gains, long-term stock investing.	Low once invested; requires discipline.	Extremely high when compounded over years.
Rental Income	Rental Income (Secondary)	Income from property or assets people pay to use.	Renting equipment, sub-leasing items, future real estate.	Medium - some management required.	High once scaled.
Royalty Income	Royalty Income (Secondary)	Income from intellectual property licensing.	Books, music, software, designs, patents.	Medium upfront effort; low ongoing.	High if the asset spreads widely.
Transfer Income	Transfer Income (Secondary)	Income you receive that is not tied to work: scholarships, grants, stipends, remittances.	Scholarships, research stipends, bursaries, government grants.	Low. Based on eligibility or performance.	Low to medium; supports your journey but doesn't compound.
Speculative Income	None (High-Risk Category)	High-risk, high-volatility	Crypto trading, flipping,	Varies; emotionally	Unpredictable. Only for high-

Category of Income	Aligns To (Primary/Secondary Path)	What It Means	Examples Students Can Build	Effort Required	Long-Term Wealth Potential
		income that can grow fast or collapse instantly.	high-risk options, arbitrage.	demanding.	risk students.

Table 21. THE BASIC CATEGORIES OF INCOME

Learning to Save, not Spend, Invest & Reinvest

Learning to save rather than spend is one of the most important habits you will ever build, because it is the foundation of every future investment you make. Most students focus only on what they earn, but wealthy people focus on what they keep. Saving is not about denial; it is about positioning yourself to take advantage of opportunities when they appear. When you choose not to spend on things that lose value the moment you buy them, you create the financial space to invest in things that grow. Many genuinely wealthy people live modestly because they understand this principle at a deep level. They are not interested in showing off, they are interested in accumulating appreciating assets that work for them over time. When you spend less, it is exactly the same as earning more, because the gap between your income and expenses becomes your investment fuel.

Once you begin saving consistently, the next step is to invest and reinvest. This is where compounding changes your life. Compounding means that the money you invest earns returns, and then those returns also begin to earn returns. Over time, your money starts working harder than you do, accelerating your wealth far beyond what simple saving could ever achieve. A student who invests small amounts early, even ten or twenty dollars a week, will often end up with far more wealth than someone who waits until they have a high salary. The habit of reinvesting your profits, rather than spending them, is the key to turning small beginnings into large outcomes. Wealthy people follow this model relentlessly, always prioritizing assets that appreciate rather than objects that drain money and attention.

Table 22 provides a simple summary table of the core principles you need to internalize, if you wish to be rich student, laying the foundation for a wealthy life.

Table 22. CORE PRINCIPLES FOR BUILDING LONG TERM WEALTH

Principle	What It Means	Why It Matters for You
Spending on Appreciating and Producing Assets	Directing money away from items that lose value and toward assets that grow or generate income.	Every dollar you avoid wasting becomes investment fuel that increases your long-term net worth.
Compounding	Your returns generate their own returns, creating accelerating growth over time.	Small, consistent investments can grow into large sums because your money is working even when you are not.
Investing in the Path That Maximizes Your Advantages	Choosing income and investment routes aligned with your competitive, comparative, and collaborative strengths.	You earn more, learn faster, and compound quicker when you build in the areas where you already have natural or developed advantages.
Rate of Return	The percentage gain your investments achieve each year.	Even small increases in return lead to huge differences when compounded for years, making this one of the most critical wealth drivers.
Time Horizon	The length of time you leave your investments to grow.	The earlier you start and the longer you stay invested, the more compounding accelerates your wealth.
Risk–Return Alignment	Matching the level of risk you take to your goals, age, and tolerance.	Taking too little risk limits growth and taking too much risk can wipe out progress. Balanced decisions keep you moving forward safely.

Setting Your Personal Income Goals and Targets

Setting your personal income goals and targets begins with understanding what you need and what you genuinely want. For some of you, the goal will be modest. You might simply want supplementary income to make your student life more comfortable, to cover weekly expenses, or to reduce the financial pressure on your family. If this is your starting point, your targets might be small but meaningful, such as earning an extra fifty to one hundred dollars a week through micro-tasks, tutoring, or small business activities. For others, the goal is more ambitious. You might want to cover your full cost of living, including your accommodation, food, transport, and course fees. Many undergraduate and master's students fall into this category, especially those without external support. Here you must think differently, mapping out exactly how much you need to earn each month so that you can sustain yourself without sinking into debt.

Beyond these two groups are those who see their student years not merely as a survival phase but as a launchpad. Your targets are not about getting by but getting ahead. Some of the world's wealthiest and most influential people used their student years to build something unique before the world even knew their name. Bill Gates, Steve Jobs, Mark Zuckerberg, and many others left education early or pursued unconventional paths because they were frustrated by slow learning, rigid systems, and environments that did not match their ambition. I felt the same. I did not want to wait to become an employee or a consumer. I wanted to produce. If this resonates with you, then your income goals will be broader, future-oriented, and tied to building an asset or business, something that compounds far beyond your immediate living costs.

To choose your goals realistically, you need clear criteria that help you think through what kind of future you want and how fast you want to move toward it. Your goals depend on your starting point, your risk appetite, your competitive, comparative, and collaborative advantages, and the kind of income streams you want to build. Most importantly, they depend on whether you want to stay level with your life or break ahead of it.

Student 1

Student 1 is the student who already has part of their fees or living costs covered by family support, scholarships, or loans, and simply needs a supplementary income to make student life easier. Their goals are modest, focused on covering small shortfalls, reducing financial stress, and giving themselves a bit more breathing room each month. This student is not aiming to build a business or generate large profits yet. Their targets are practical and achievable (See Table 23 below) through flexible, low-pressure income streams that fit around their studies, allowing them to focus on stability and consistency rather than high levels of risk or ambition.

Category	Annual Cost	Covered by Family/Loans	Income You Need to Earn
Table 23. STUDENTS SEEKING SUPPLEMENTARY INCOME ONLY			
Tuition fees	$10,000	$10,000	$0
Accommodation	$5,000	$3,000	$2,000
Food	$2,000	$1,000	$1,000
Transport & essentials	$1,000	$500	$500
Total Required Income			**$3,500 per year** (approx. $70 per week)

Student 2

Student 2 must cover the full cost of their education, accommodation, food, and essentials through their own effort. There is no external financial cushion, so their income targets need to be clear, disciplined, and reliable. This student requires a structured approach, combining earned income with small entrepreneurial activities that deliver predictable weekly and monthly returns. Their goal is survival without falling into debt, which demands careful planning, smart use of time, and a willingness to take on income streams that can scale slightly as their confidence and capability grow. (See Table 24 below).

Category	Annual Cost	External Help	Income You Need to Earn
Table 24. STUDENTS WHO MUST COVER ALL THEIR LIVING COSTS			
Tuition fees	$10,000	$0	$10,000
Accommodation	$5,000	$0	$5,000
Food	$2,000	$0	$2,000
Transport & essentials	$1,000	$0	$1,000
Total Required Income			**$18,000 per year** (approx. $350 per week)

Student 3

Student 3 sees their student years not as a holding pattern but as a launchpad. They want to cover all their costs, but their ambitions extend far beyond that. Their target is to generate surplus income (See Table 25 below), invest in assets, test ideas, and build momentum toward long-term wealth. This student is actively looking for a "widget", a scalable product, service, or business model that can grow significantly with time, reinvestment, and effort. Their goals are aspirational rather than minimal, and their plan reflects a desire to move ahead of the pack, using their competitive, comparative, and collaborative advantages to accelerate their financial future while still studying.

Table 25.	STUDENTS WHO WANT TO BUILD WEALTH AND LEAP AHEAD		
Category	**Annual Cost**	**Covered by Income Streams**	**Desired Extra Income for Growth**
Tuition + living	$17,000	$17,000	$0
Wealth-building investments	–	–	$5,000–$20,000
Business development budget	–	–	$1,000–$10,000
Total Target Income			**$22,000–$47,000 per year**

This section should have helped you to think through how you build your personal income strategy framework. Once you define your income goals and targets clearly, you will know exactly what you are aiming for, how much you need to earn, and which income strategies that follow in this chapter are right for you. From here, you will be able to create a personalized, actionable plan that bridges the gap between where you are today and the financial future you want to build.

Build Your Very Own Income Strategy Framework

Building your own income strategy framework means taking everything you have learned so far, stepping back, and translating it into a clear, personal plan.

You are moving from theory to action, and the goal is simple: understand exactly who you are, your own unique starting point, what you have at your disposal, and where you want to go. As noted above, every student's situation is different. Some of you want small supplementary income, some need to cover all your costs, and others are using these years as a launchpad to get ahead. Your framework helps you map your own position, your advantages, your constraints, and your ambition.

To complete your framework, work through each section honestly. Identify the income strategies that match your competitive, comparative, and collaborative advantages. Be clear about your risk appetite, your short-term needs, and your long-term vision. The framework exists to help you see the whole picture: who you are today, the opportunities around you, and the steps you will take next. This is not about copying anyone else's plan but about building the one that fits your reality.

Once you fill it in, you will have a personalized blueprint that shows how you will move from poor student to rich student, from survival to independence, and from drifting to deliberate action. This becomes the basis for your own income strategy moving forward.

How Long Will It Take Me to Produce my Own Income Strategy Framework?

A book like this is not something to rush through. It is short enough to finish quickly, but powerful enough that it deserves time, reflection, and repeated return. A good student will read it slowly over the course of a month, pausing often to think about their starting point, their strengths, their disadvantages, their desires, and the assets they already have at their disposal. The purpose is not to build your income strategy in a single sitting and then forget about it. Your framework is a living document, something you update, refine, adjust and rebuild as you learn, as you grow, and as your confidence increases.

If you treat it seriously, it will become a personal compass. You set targets, track progress, stay focused on your core values, and avoid the traps that keep most people poor. The biggest trap is earning money only to spend it immediately on something that loses value. The discipline of putting your money back into appreciating assets or into your next income step is what builds long term stability. This discipline creates a financial buffer in your life, which in turn creates freedom, reduces stress, and lets you sleep easily without worrying about the next bill or the next crisis.

There is no fixed timeline for mastering this. Some students might build their strategy in a few months; others may take a year or two. What matters is that you commit to the process, keep updating it, and keep moving. If you do that, this framework will become one of the most valuable tools you carry into the rest of your life.

Table 26 is your personal blueprint for moving from uncertainty to a clear, practical income strategy that fits your identity, your skills, and your goals. It breaks the entire process into simple steps, helping you map out where you are today, what advantages you can use, and how you will build income over the next days, weeks, and months. This matters for students because it turns vague ambition into a structured plan you can act on immediately, giving you direction, momentum, and a realistic pathway from being a poor student to becoming a rich student.

Table 26. YOUR PERSONAL INCOME STRATEGY FRAMEWORK		
Section	**What You Need to Write**	**Examples to Guide You**
1. Who You Are	Your identity, strengths, personality, interests and long-term purpose.	I'm creative and communicate well." "I want independence and a flexible career."
2. Your Starting Point	Your current situation: location, finances, networks, skills and constraints.	"Live in shared housing, limited savings." "Small town but good internet."
3. Skills You Already Have	Skills you can use immediately to earn income.	"Basic design skills." "Good at math and explaining concepts."
4. Assets and Resources You Control	Tools, equipment, spaces or relationships you can use.	"Laptop, smartphone, access to a family workshop."
5. Your Competitive Advantage	What you do better than most people around you.	"I can edit videos fast." "I'm persuasive in selling."
6. Your Comparative Advantage	What you can do with less effort, cost or time than others.	"Tutoring is easy for me." "I can make social posts quickly."
7. Your Collaborative Advantage	Who you can partner with to multiply results.	"Friend who codes." "Classmate with photography skills."

Table 26. YOUR PERSONAL INCOME STRATEGY FRAMEWORK

Section	What You Need to Write	Examples to Guide You
8. Your Risk Appetite	How much uncertainty you can tolerate financially and emotionally.	"Low risk, prefer stable income streams." "High risk, willing to experiment aggressively."
9. Your Income Goal (Short-Term)	What you want to earn in the next 3–6 months.	"$300–$500 per month."
10. Your Income Goal (Medium-Term)	What you want in the next 1–2 years.	"$1,000/month digital income."
11. Your Income Goal (Long-Term)	What you want by age 25, 30 or beyond.	"Financial independence with multiple streams."
12. Your Time Availability	Hours per week you can commit.	"10 hours during term, 20 during holidays."
13. Your Market Environment	Whether your best market is local, digital or global.	"Local demand low, online demand high."
14. Problems You Can Solve	Real problems people pay to remove.	"Students need CV support." "Businesses need TikTok content."
15. Opportunities You Can Enter Quickly	Ideas you can start within 7 days.	"Tutoring, reselling, editing reels."
16. Your Main Income Strategy Choice	The primary strategy that best fits your context.	"Freelance design + micro digital products."
17. Your Secondary Strategy (Optional)	Backup or low-effort pathway.	"Flip items on Marketplace."
18. First Three Actions (Next 48 Hours)	Concrete steps you will take immediately.	"Message 10 clients." "Create 3 sample designs."
19. First Week Plan	What you will achieve in 7 days.	"Portfolio ready, sample work posted."
20. First Month Plan	Your target achievements for the first month.	"First 3 paying clients, $150 earned."
21. How You Will Scale	How you will grow from student income to independence.	"Automate tasks, raise prices, build digital products."
22. Long-Term Investment Path	How earnings transition into saving and investing.	"Save $1,000, invest in ETFs, build emergency fund."
23. Your Final Vision	The lifestyle and independence you are building toward.	"Graduate already earning, debt-free, building a scalable business."

Why AI Will Accelerate Your Income Strategy

Before you move into the next chapter and explore the full list of income ideas, you need to understand one of the biggest forces reshaping the world you are about to enter. Artificial intelligence is no longer a distant concept or a specialist tool used by a few. It is rapidly becoming the single greatest accelerator available to students, entrepreneurs, creators, and anyone who wants to build income with limited resources. AI has changed the cost of experimentation, the speed of learning, the volume of output you can produce, and the quality you can achieve before you even graduate.

Where previous generations needed teams, capital, or years of experience to achieve scale, you now have tools that allow you to design, build, analyze, research, market, and produce at a fraction of the time and cost. AI collapses barriers that once defined the limits of student entrepreneurship. You can create prototypes in minutes, generate professional-level content without hiring designers, test market demand instantly, and support clients with the kind of speed and precision that was impossible even three years ago. These changes reshape the entire logic of choosing an income strategy. Risk falls, timelines shorten, learning curves flatten, and your ability to scale increases sharply.

More importantly, AI does not replace students, it replaces students who choose not to use it. Those who adopt it become faster, more accurate, more creative, and more competitive in every income category. Immediate-return ideas become easier to start. Short-term ideas become more profitable. Medium-term projects can be built with fewer people. Long-term ventures become more ambitious and more realistic. AI is not a separate path, it is the amplifier sitting beneath every path you are about to consider.

Understanding this shift prepares you for the next chapter. Several of the income ideas have been rewritten specifically for an AI-driven world. Many traditional ideas have new life because AI strengthens them. And entirely new opportunities exist that previous generations could not access. Consider this your final mental upgrade before you dive into the practical toolkit. You now understand identity, abundance, business, money, and opportunity. AI is the accelerator that ties these ideas together and propels you forward.

Rich Student. Poor Student.

With this in mind, you are ready to turn the page and explore one hundred practical strategies that any student can begin immediately, each one shaped for a world where AI is part of the landscape you will soon compete and thrive in.

10. LIVING FULLY – EARNING MONEY AND GIVING BACK

How Wealth Becomes Freedom, and Freedom Becomes Service

L iving fully begins with understanding that life is not a rehearsal. Every choice shapes your freedom, every action shapes your future, and every breath is a reminder that time is precious. To live fully is to develop the skills, insight, and independence that allow you to take care of yourself, contribute to others, and play your part in building a peaceful and compassionate society. Money is part of that journey, but only part. It is a tool, never the destination. What truly matters is how you grow, how you use what you earn, and how you give what you can.

At the heart of living fully is the understanding that personal freedom comes from competence. When you know how to earn, manage, and grow your resources, you are no longer pushed about by circumstance. You gain choices. You gain dignity. You gain the ability to stand on your own feet. This is why learning about money, investment, and business matters for every young person. Not for luxury, not for ego, but for freedom. The world has always been divided into three broad groups, those who take care of themselves and others, those who manage to take care of themselves but cannot support others, and those who need the support of society to survive. A strong society needs all three, but it also needs more people who have the skills and confidence to build businesses, create value, and lead with generosity.

At the moment, something is missing. Too many communities suffer not from a shortage of compassion but from a shortage of practical knowledge about how to start, grow, and sustain enterprises that create jobs and opportunity. Many young people have passion without a plan, dreams without tools, enthusiasm without guidance. To live fully is to close that gap. It means learning how the world of work and money functions. It means seeing business as a force that can expand wellbeing, not simply wealth. It means understanding that the goal is not to hoard, but to circulate value in ways that strengthen the whole.

Living fully also means cultivating the inner qualities that allow you to thrive. Awareness. Discipline. Kind hearted intentions. A sense of higher purpose. When these qualities guide your actions, you will not be driven only by consumption or comparison. You will measure your life not by what you have, but by what you contribute. You will understand that generosity begins with clarity and that real success is the ability to make choices that uplift others as well as yourself. True wealth is the ability to say yes when you want to help, and to have the capacity to make that help meaningful.

Giving back is not something that waits until later in life. It is part of the cycle from the beginning. Every time you help someone understand something that took you years to learn, you give back. Every time you share your strength, your time, your ideas, you give back. Every time you use your skills to build something that benefits more than just yourself, you give back. This is the cycle of life. You grow so that you can lift. You earn so that you can contribute. You rise so that you can raise others.

And for me, this is not theoretical. I have travelled twenty to twenty-five countries a year for two decades, advising governments and businesses on investments measured in trillions. I own property across three continents. I run two companies. I began on a building site with nothing. I am a self-made multi-millionaire, yet the sum of me fits into my ideas, my laptop, my phones, and a suitcase. I rarely live in the homes I own.

Artificial intelligence will also expand your ability to contribute. By freeing you from repetitive tasks and giving you greater leverage over your time, AI allows you to focus more on the parts of life that genuinely matter. You can teach, mentor, support causes, volunteer digitally, build tools that help others, or create products that serve people far beyond your immediate environment. With the right intention, AI becomes a multiplier for compassion and impact, enabling you to give more, reach more, and lift more people as your capacity grows.

I use little of the wealth I have generated for me. Most of it serves other purposes, including a new startup dedicated to solving the global crisis in refugee shelter and housing. Living fully has taught me that the more successful people become, the greater their capacity to give back. That is the purpose of this chapter, and the purpose of every lesson ahead, to help you earn well, live freely, and contribute generously to a world that needs the very best of you.

Table 27 gives you an overview of how taking out and giving back work together to create the virtuous cycle described earlier in the book. Taking out allows you to build skills, assets, confidence, and independence by drawing value from the economy. Giving back completes the loop by returning value to your family, your community, and the wider systems that enabled your success. When you practice both sides deliberately, you turn personal growth into collective strength, and each round of taking out and giving back reinforces the next. This is how a virtuous cycle emerges, where the more you rise, the more you are able to lift others, and the more your contribution strengthens the world you depend on.

Table 27. TAKING OUT VS GIVING BACK	
Taking Out	**Giving Back**
Extracting value from the economy through work, enterprise, or investment	Circulating value back into families, communities, and the wider world
Using your skills, time, energy, and intention to generate personal income	Using your income, insight, and influence to strengthen others
Benefiting from industries and systems that create opportunity	Repairing, restoring, or improving the same systems so others can benefit too

Table 27. TAKING OUT VS GIVING BACK	
Taking Out	**Giving Back**
Turning knowledge, experience, and ambition into personal progress	Sharing knowledge, mentoring others, and helping people grow faster than you did
Building financial capacity, independence, and resilience	Using that capacity to support your family, fund ideas, and uplift the vulnerable
Taking resources from the world, including environmental and social systems	Protecting the environment, supporting social causes, and reinvesting in communities
Growing assets, savings, skills, and networks	Expanding access, opportunity, and dignity for others through your actions
Extracting wealth from the marketplace	Returning wealth ethically to society through service, philanthropy, and meaningful work

The next chapter brings this mindset to life. Chapter 11 presents one hundred short, medium, and longer-term ideas you can explore, adapt, or build from. They are not prescriptions, they are prompts, designed to elevate your sense of possibility and strengthen the freedom that comes from seeing opportunity everywhere."

11. 100 IDEAS FOR STUDENT INCOME STREAMS

A Trigger List for Building Your Own Path to Income and Wealth

This chapter is not a list of instructions you must follow, nor is it a catalogue of perfect ideas waiting for you to copy. In fact, many of the one hundred ideas that follow may not interest you at all. That is not the point. The value of this chapter is that by reading through a wide range of possibilities, you begin to understand the sheer diversity of ways that income can be created, captured, and scaled. Some ideas may spark your imagination, others may sharpen your sense of what you do not want, and a few may fit your strengths perfectly.

See these ideas as triggers, prompts, and exemplars, not as a checklist. Dip into them whenever you need inspiration or perspective. The purpose is to open your thinking, widen your field of vision, and help you recognize how you might strengthen your own income and wealth future. Use these examples as reference points, as catalysts for your creativity, and as reminders that opportunity exists everywhere once you learn how to look for it.

Immediate-Return Business Ideas (1–25)

Immediate-return business ideas are the fastest way for you to start earning money while you study. These ideas require minimal setup, low risk, and almost no capital, allowing you to generate income within days rather than months. They are practical, flexible, and designed to fit around your academic schedule. Some may only earn small amounts, others may grow into something larger, but each one teaches you how to create value quickly, test the market, and build confidence through action.

Table 28 gives you a fast, practical overview of income ideas that can start paying you almost immediately. Each option requires little setup, low risk, and skills many students already have, making it ideal for anyone who wants to earn money this week rather than months from now. This matters because early wins build confidence, create momentum, and give you the cash you need to save, invest, or fund the next stage of your income strategy. Each of the ideas summarized in this table is explained in fuller detail in the sections that follow, giving you clear guidance on how to start, what you need, and how each option can work for you as a student.

No.	Title	Main Description	Is This Right for You?
	Table 28. SUMMARY IMMEDIATE-RETURN BUSINESS IDEAS		
1	AI-augmented freelancing	Create high-quality written, visual or research content by combining your skills with AI tools.	Strong writing or design ability; basic laptop; ideal for students wanting fast, flexible income.
2	Freelance Graphic Design	Logos, posters, social media assets	Design skill; basic laptop; small campus clients to begin
3	Web Development	Build sites or troubleshoot code	Coding basics; portfolio; no capital needed
4	AI-Supported Tutoring	Academic tutoring using AI to personalize study materials	Subject mastery; confidence teaching; AI tools to enhance learning; zero cost
5	Pet Sitting & Dog Walking	Walk pets or sit animals	Love animals; local customers; flexible time
6	Babysitting	Child care evenings/weekends	Responsible; trusted; earns cash quickly

Table 28. SUMMARY IMMEDIATE-RETURN BUSINESS IDEAS

No.	Title	Main Description	Is This Right for You?
7	House Cleaning	Clean dorms, flats, houses	Low-cost supplies; discipline; immediate cash
8	House Sitting	Look after homes during absences	Trustworthy; minimal effort; paid to be present
9	Lawn/Yard Care	Mowing, raking, snow removal	Physical work; basic tools; strong local demand
10	Tech or Repair Services	Phone, laptop, furniture repairs	Basic technical skill; small toolkit
11	Rideshare/Delivery	Driving or cycling deliveries	Car or bike; app sign-up; steady income
12	Selling Used Items	Flip textbooks, clothes, electronics	Sharp eye for value; small initial stock
13	Thrift/Furniture Flipping	Refurbish and resell items	Creativity; pickup/transport access
14	Selling Handmade Crafts	Jeweler, art, gifts on campus	Craft skill; small materials cost
15	Baking & Cooking	Bake goods or meal boxes	Kitchen access; simple ingredients; strong student demand
16	Event Photography	Take photos/videos at events	Camera; editing basics; fast delivery
17	Personal Training & Fitness	Fitness coaching or classes	Fitness skill; confidence; campus gym
18	Grooming & Beauty	Haircuts, makeup, nails	Skill-based; low-cost kit; consistent clients
19	Errands & Odd Jobs	Groceries, line-waiting, chores	Reliable; flexible time; quick payouts
20	AI-Driven Research & Analysis	Summaries, insights, comparisons using AI tools	Internet access; analytical mindset; fast, high-value task delivery
21	Printing Services	Print essays, flyers, packets	Printer; late-night availability; small but steady
22	Mystery Shopping	Store evaluations or app testing	Attention to detail; small tasks; simple payouts
23	Renting Out Your Stuff	Bikes, cameras, calculators	Own useful items; set fees; easy passive income

No.	Title	Main Description	Is This Right for You?
24	Campus Services	Laundry, move-in/out help	Understand student pain points; low capital
25	Credit Reward Arbitrage	Cashback and bonuses	Discipline with money; only works if debt-free

Table 28. SUMMARY IMMEDIATE-RETURN BUSINESS IDEAS

1. AI-augmented freelancing. This allows you to earn immediately by combining your writing, design, research, or communication skills with AI tools to deliver high-quality work at exceptional speed. Instead of spending hours drafting, editing, or creating visuals manually, you use AI to generate structured outlines, refine text, produce design concepts, analyze information, and accelerate repetitive tasks. You then apply your judgement to polish and personalize the final output. This gives clients professional-level results faster than traditional freelancers can deliver.

You can find gigs on freelancing platforms, through social media, or by approaching local businesses that need support with content, design, branding, marketing material, pitch decks, reports, or research summaries. Many small companies cannot afford agencies, but will readily pay for fast, reliable, AI-enhanced support from a capable student. A growing number of young freelancers now use AI to produce blogs, social posts, business plans, product descriptions, and visual assets in a fraction of the time it once took. For example, many student freelancers have built full digital studios from their laptops, using AI to complete work that previously required small teams.

Return horizon: Immediate. You are paid per project, per deliverable, or on short retainers once clients see the quality and turnaround speed you offer. This makes AI-augmented freelancing one of the fastest and most scalable income streams available to students, enabling you to earn, learn, and build a portfolio far more efficiently than traditional freelancing pathways.

2. Freelance Graphic Design: Use design talent to create logos, social media graphics, or marketing materials for paying clients. Many small businesses and student organizations need affordable design help. You can start by advertising on campus or freelancing sites and get paid per design project. *Return horizon: Immediate.* Each completed project yields immediate income. (For instance, a design student who took on logo commissions in college not only earned money but also built a portfolio for future opportunities.)

3. Freelance Web Development or Coding: Turn coding skills into cash by building websites or apps for others. Even simple sites for local businesses or student clubs can earn a quick fee. Many companies seek part-time web developers for short tasks or debugging. *Return horizon: Immediate.* You typically receive payment as soon as the site or feature is delivered. (One computer science student taught himself web development and earned money creating websites for local businesses, getting paid per project and building experience for a tech career.)

4. AI-Supported Tutoring: Earn money by tutoring school or college students in subjects you excel at, but with the added advantage of using AI to personalize lessons, generate practice questions and simplify complex ideas. You can charge hourly rates for one-on-one or small-group sessions, offering faster and more tailored support than traditional tutors. AI allows you to prepare materials quickly, diagnose weak areas and build structured revision plans, making your sessions more effective and attractive to students. Return horizon: Immediate. Each session or weekly block provides instant income. For example, a student tutor could combine their subject knowledge with AI-generated quizzes and explanations, helping learners progress faster and increasing demand for their services. With this model, many students expand from solo tutoring into small tutoring ventures, offering premium, AI-enhanced support that stands out from standard academic help.

5. Pet Sitting and Dog Walking: Busy pet owners will pay you to walk their dogs or watch their pets. This requires little startup cost—just reliability and love for animals. Apps like Rover or simply flyers in your neighborhood can connect you with gigs. *Return horizon: Immediate.* You get paid per walk or pet-sitting job, often the same day or week. As an example, Reported examples include NYU student Emma Purcell, who has described earning in the range of approximately $14–$24 per dog walk through platforms such as Rover.

6. Babysitting and Child Care: Offer babysitting services during evenings or weekends. Parents in college towns or faculty with young children often need trustworthy sitters. You can earn hourly and often in cash. *Return horizon: Immediate.* Payment usually occurs at the end of each babysitting shift. In fact, some students have **paid a significant part of their college expenses through babysitting income] . It's a fast way to earn money, and building a good reputation can keep the referrals coming.

7. House Cleaning Services: Start a simple cleaning service for dorms, apartments, or local homes. Many people are willing to pay students to do cleaning, organizing, or odd household chores. You can schedule cleanings around classes and get paid per job. *Return horizon: Immediate.* Each cleaning job provides immediate cash upon completion. One well-documented example is Hannah Teschler, a Baylor University student who founded Mop Mob LLC as a small college cleaning venture, which quickly scaled beyond campus demand. She started with a small summer cleaning gig that paid her right away and then rapidly scaled it up.

8. House Sitting: Get paid to watch over someone's home (and sometimes pets) while they're away. Responsibilities might include collecting mail, watering plants, or just being on-site for security. House sitting often pays by the day or week. *Return horizon: Immediate.* You typically receive payment as soon as the homeowner returns. (For instance, some students in vacation towns line up house-sitting jobs during holidays and earn quick income for minimal work – effectively getting paid to stay in someone's home.)

9. Lawn Care and Yard Work: Offer lawn mowing, raking leaves, snow shoveling, gardening, or general yard maintenance services. Neighbors often prefer hiring an enterprising student over professional landscapers for basic tasks. You can earn cash the same day you work. *Return horizon: Immediate.* Payment is usually

Peter J. Middlebrook

provided upon completing the job. (One enterprising student spent weekends mowing lawns in his community – charging per yard – and used the cash earned each week to cover his groceries and save for bigger goals.)

10. Handyperson or Tech Repair Services: If you're handy with tools or tech, offer quick fix-it services. This could include assembling IKEA furniture, fixing bikes, or doing minor phone/computer repairs for a fee. Many classmates or locals will gladly pay for help fixing a cracked phone screen or removing a virus from a laptop. *Return horizon: Immediate.* Clients pay at the time of service. (For example, a tech-savvy student advertised phone repair services on campus – replacing cracked screens in an hour – and earned money immediately per repair. His affordable, fast service gained him a loyal customer base among peers.)

11. Rideshare and Delivery Gigs: Use your car (or bike) to earn by driving for Uber or Lyft, or delivering food with apps like DoorDash and UberEats, provided it's allowed in your area and you meet the age requirements. You can work whenever you have free time. *Return horizon: Immediate.* These apps pay out weekly or even daily (with instant pay options). A student with a car can, for example, spend a few hours each evening delivering food and bring in cash tips plus earnings the same week – a quick infusion of income that can be saved or used to fund other ventures.

12. Selling Used Items (Flipping Textbooks and More): Turn clutter into cash by selling things you don't need – textbooks, clothes, electronics – on marketplaces like Facebook, eBay, or campus bulletin boards. You can also scour thrift stores or clearance sales for undervalued items and resell them at a profit. *Return horizon: Immediate.* Each sale generates immediate money. Many students recoup textbook costs by reselling them each semester; some even buy extra used textbooks from peers and resell online for profit, creating a mini book-flipping business that pays out right after each sale.

13. Thrift-Flipping and Furniture Flipping: Acquire second-hand goods or free furniture, give them a little refurbishment or cleaning, and resell them for a higher price. Students moving out often give away furniture or appliances – you can fix these up and sell to incoming students. This hustle yields quick one-time profits item by item. *Return horizon: Immediate.* As soon as an item is sold, you earn money. In one reported case, a furniture flipper referred to as Andrea described earning over $4,000 in profit in a single month by refurbishing and reselling second-hand furniture. Even smaller scale, flipping a desk or mini-fridge can put cash in your pocket within days.

14. Selling Handmade Crafts Locally: If you have a creative hobby – making jewelry, art, soaps, baked goods, etc. – sell your creations to classmates or at local markets. Many students set up small tables on campus or use Instagram to advertise their crafts. You earn cash with each sale. *Return horizon: Immediate.* Each item sold brings in money on the spot. (For instance, one student artisan started selling handmade beaded jewelry in the student center and dorm events; she earned immediate income and eventually used the proceeds to launch an online Etsy store.)

15. Baking or Cooking for Profit: Turn your kitchen skills into a micro-business. You might bake cookies, cupcakes, or prepare homemade meal boxes and sell them to busy fellow students. Some students take orders for birthday cakes or cultural home-cooked meals for those missing a taste of home. *Return horizon: Immediate.* Customers usually pay upon delivery of the food. (One student known for her baking started selling $1 brownies in her dorm; she would sell out a batch within hours, earning cash that same day, and scaled up by taking special orders for events.)

16. Event Photography or Videography: If you have a decent camera and an eye for photos, offer your services at student events, club gatherings, or birthday parties. Students will pay for quality graduation photos, headshots, or event highlight videos. You can charge per session or per event. *Return horizon: Immediate.* Photographers often get paid at the event or when delivering the final images shortly after. (For example, a student photographer charged seniors $50 each for graduation photo shoots – with 10 clients over a weekend, he earned $500, all paid upon delivering edited photos within a few days.)

17. Personal Training or Fitness Coaching: If you're knowledgeable in fitness or certified as a trainer, coach fellow students at the campus gym or nearby park for a fee. You can offer one-on-one training, bootcamps, or yoga classes. Many students prefer an affordable peer trainer over an expensive professional. *Return horizon: Immediate.* Trainers are usually paid per session or weekly. (One college athlete, for instance, began offering morning bootcamp classes for $5 per student and often had 10–15 students attend. He collected payments after each class – an immediate stream of income – while helping others get in shape.)

18. Beauty and Grooming Services: Use your skills in hair, makeup, or grooming to earn cash from your peers. Students often cut hair, do manicures, or offer makeup services for events right out of their dorm. You might charge much less than a salon, attracting budget-conscious classmates. *Return horizon: Immediate.* Clients pay when the service is done. A commonly cited example is that of Carmella Taitt, a student hairstylist who reportedly grew a dorm-based grooming side hustle to roughly a few hundred dollars per month through word-of-mouth referrals. Each haircut or makeover session put cash directly in her hand.

19. Running Errands and Odd Jobs: Offer yourself as a "taskrunner" for miscellaneous chores – picking up groceries, standing in line for event tickets, assembling furniture, or doing laundry. Busy students or local residents might prefer hiring you over doing it themselves. You can set an hourly rate or flat fee per task. *Return horizon: Immediate.* Payment is rendered as soon as the errand is completed. (For example, a student used a campus Facebook group to advertise errand services; one week he might earn $50 assembling a neighbor's bookshelf and $30 delivering groceries to a faculty member – cash earned immediately after each task.)

20. AI-Driven Research and Content Analysis: In spare minutes, use AI tools to help individuals or small organizations extract insights from documents, summarize information, and produce clear, structured reports. Instead of low-paying micro tasks, you use AI to scan articles, policy papers, interviews or datasets and turn them into concise summaries or comparisons that save clients time. This work is far more valuable and pays better than basic online gigs. Return horizon: Immediate. Many small businesses, researchers and professors need quick analysis for projects and will pay per report or summary. For example, a student might use AI to produce a two-page briefing from a long research paper and charge $15–$25 – completing the task in under an hour and earning far more than standard micro tasks.

21. Printing and Copy Services: If you have a printer or easy access to cheap copies, offer to print out essays, flyers, or class notes for a small fee (especially late at night when campus facilities might be closed). Many students will gladly pay you rather than trek to the library or print shop. Similarly, you could bind notes or create study packets and charge for those. *Return horizon: Immediate.* You collect money upon delivering the printed materials. (One student entrepreneur kept a high-quality printer in his dorm and charged classmates a few cents per page – he wasn't getting rich, but he made quick snack money every day and recouped his printing costs quickly.)

22. Mystery Shopping and User Testing: Get paid to pose as a customer or test products. Some companies pay shoppers to visit stores and report on customer service or product displays. Similarly, user-testing websites pay you to record your experience using an app or site. These gigs are sporadic but pay right after completion. *Return horizon: Immediate.* Each assignment yields a payment (often within days via direct deposit or gift cards). (For example, a student might do a mystery shop at a local cafe for $20 and a 20-minute website test for $15 on the same day – earning $35 in a day's spare time, paid shortly thereafter.)

23. Renting Out Your Stuff: Turn your possessions into assets by renting them to others. Extra bike sitting around? Rent it out for a weekend. Got a graphing calculator, musical instrument, or camera not in use? Other students might pay a small fee to borrow it rather than buying their own. There are even apps for peer-to-peer rentals. *Return horizon: Immediate.* You receive rental fees upfront or when the item is returned. (One student photographer rented out his DSLR camera to a classmate for a project at $15/day – an easy $45 when it was returned after 3 days, effectively making money off an idle asset.)

24. Campus-Specific Services (Laundry, Moving Help, etc.): Identify everyday headaches for students and solve them for a fee. This could be doing laundry for busy peers (charge per load), offering dorm move-in/out help at semester changes, or cleaning dorm common areas on weekends. These are things students might dislike doing and gladly outsource to you. *Return horizon: Immediate.* You're paid at the time of service. For instance, a pair of students started a "laundry pick-up" service in their residence hall – they charged a few dollars per load and collected cash from classmates each week, turning a chore into an immediate income source.

25. Credit Card Rewards Arbitrage: (Proceed with caution.) If used responsibly, take advantage of student credit card sign-up bonuses or cashback programs to earn money or free travel. Some cards offer $100+ bonuses or points for signing up and meeting a minimum spend (which you can achieve by paying your routine bills, then paying off the card). Additionally, using a cashback card for your regular expenses essentially "pays" you a percentage back. *Return horizon: Immediate (for bonuses) to Short-Term.* For example, a student might get a credit card with a $200 cashback bonus after spending $500 on groceries and books (expenses they had anyway) – they meet the requirement within a month and receive $200 cashback. Important: This only builds wealth if you use cards wisely (always pay in full to avoid interest); otherwise, debt interest would wipe out the benefits.

Short-Term Business Ideas (Weeks to Months, 26–50)
Short-term business ideas take a little longer to build, but they offer far greater potential and flexibility. These ideas usually require several weeks or a few months of consistent effort to set up, refine, and gain traction. They often involve building a small product, service, or

online presence that can generate repeat income once it starts working. While the payoff is not immediate, the returns can be far higher than the quick-win ideas, and the learning curve is invaluable. These are the kinds of projects that grow your skills, expand your confidence, and begin shifting you from simple earning to real entrepreneurship.

Table 29 gives you a clear overview of short-term business ideas that take a little longer to build but offer far greater potential once they gain momentum. These ideas require some planning, consistency, and skill development, yet they are perfect for students who want to move beyond quick cash and begin creating income streams that can grow over weeks and months. This matters because short-term ideas help you transition from immediate earnings to structured ventures that can scale, strengthen your portfolio, and prepare you for long-term wealth building. Each of the ideas summarized in this table is explained in fuller detail in the sections that follow, giving you clear guidance on how to start, what you need, and how each option can work for you as a student.

Table 29.	SUMMARY OF SHORT-TERM BUSINESS IDEAS		
No.	Title	Main Description	Is This Right for You?
26	AI-Accelerated E-Commerce	Use AI to design products, test ideas and launch online stores without inventory	Creative; small startup budget; ideal for students wanting fast, scalable online business
27	Dropshipping Store	Sell products shipped by suppliers so you never touch inventory	Basic marketing; social media ads; small setup budget
28	Affiliate Marketing	Promote products and earn commissions on clicks or sales	Build an audience early; steady posting; no capital
29	Social Media Influencer	Build a niche following and earn from ads, partnerships, creator funds	Strong personality or theme; consistent posting
30	Digital Product Sales	E-books, templates, planners, stock photos, guides	Create once; sell repeatedly; no manufacturing cost
31	Subscription Box	Monthly themed boxes curated for a niche group	Curating products; small upfront sourcing budget

No.	Title	Main Description	Is This Right for You?
	Table 29.	**SUMMARY OF SHORT-TERM BUSINESS IDEAS**	
32	AI-Generated Digital Products	Create study packs, templates or revision materials using AI	Strong academic or creative skills; basic laptop; ideal for scalable digital work
33	Simple Apps or Websites	Build small tools or content sites earning ad revenue	Basic coding; simple idea; passive income potential
34	Event & Party Planning	Coordinate student events, birthdays, club socials	Organized; confident with people; low capital
35	CV & Cover Letter Service	Rewrite résumés, statements, job applications	Strong writing; understanding hiring expectations
36	Online Language Teaching	Teach languages to global learners on tutoring platforms	Native proficiency or strong fluency; minimal setup
37	Virtual Assistant	Manage email, scheduling, research for clients online	Reliable; organized; good communication skills
38	NFT / Digital Art Sales	Create and list digital artwork or collectibles	Artistic; speculative; requires digital platform setup
39	Catering or Meal Prep	Weekly menus, boxed meals, baked goods for students	Cooking skill; simple packaging; consistent delivery
40	Upcycled Fashion	Refurbish clothing or turn thrift items into unique pieces	Eye for design; basic sewing; thrift sourcing
41	Etsy Handmade Store	Handmade items sold globally via Etsy	Creative; small toolkits; branding focus
42	Freelance Video Editing	Edit reels, shorts, vlogs, promo videos	Editing software; sample portfolio; fast turnaround
43	Music or Art Lessons	Teach guitar, piano, singing, drawing or painting	Competent skill level; patient teaching style
44	Podcasting	Launch a niche podcast and monetize through sponsors	Clear topic; steady publishing; simple recording gear
45	Custom Clothing Line	Small-batch streetwear or printed apparel drops	Design sense; supplier access; small production runs
46	App Development Services	Build apps for small businesses or student groups	Strong coding; ability to deliver clean features

No.	Title	Main Description	Is This Right for You?
	Table 29.	**SUMMARY OF SHORT-TERM BUSINESS IDEAS**	
47	AI-Powered Micro-Agency	Use AI to manage marketing, content and online ads	Marketing interest; client skills; AI tools to scale work without a team
48	Interior Decorating	Transform dorm rooms or small apartments	Styling sense; practical layout skills; low cost
49	Campus Equipment Rental	Rent fridges, microwaves, projectors, fans	Small upfront purchase; recurring rental income
50	Vending Machine Business	Place machines with snacks or essentials in high-traffic areas	Upfront cost for machine; restocking discipline

26. AI-accelerated e-commerce: AI-accelerated e-commerce lets you use AI tools to design products, test ideas and launch online stores quickly without needing inventory or complex technical skills. You can create product visuals, ad copy, branding and market analysis using AI, then list items through platforms that handle production and shipping for you. Return horizon: Short-Term (a few weeks). Once your designs or product ideas are uploaded, you can begin earning within weeks as orders come in through your store. This approach is low-investment and highly scalable. (For example, a student could use AI to generate a unique product concept, launch it on a dropshipping or print-on-demand platform, promote it on social media, and start receiving orders within a month – earning profit on each sale without holding stock.) Results vary by niche, marketing skill, and platform fees.

27. Dropshipping E-Commerce Store: Run an online store without stocking inventory by partnering with suppliers who ship products directly to customers. You focus on creating a website (often via Shopify) and marketing products; when an order comes in, the supplier fulfils it. Many students have tried this with trending products or niche items. *Return horizon: Short-Term.* While not instantaneous, a well-marketed dropshipping store can start generating revenue in a matter of weeks. A widely reported example is Cole Turner, who has described building a dropshipping store and later reporting multi-million-dollar sales while still young. The initial profits started within a couple of months once he found what resonated with customers.

28. Affiliate Marketing: Promote other companies' products or services through special referral links and earn a commission on any sale or sign-up generated through your link. Students can do this via blogs, social media, or YouTube by reviewing products or sharing referral codes. It's especially effective if you have an online following or a niche audience (e.g. a tech review blog or a fashion Instagram). *Return horizon: Short-Term.* It may take a few weeks or months of consistent content to see significant commissions, but it can happen quickly with a viral post. In one reported case, a student affiliate marketer described earning around $10,000 in a strong month after a post gained traction.

29. Social Media Influencing (TikTok / Instagram): Build a following around entertaining or informative content and monetize it through sponsorships, brand deals, or creator funds. Short-form platforms like TikTok can explode in popularity in weeks if you hit a trend. As your follower count rises, companies may pay you to promote their products, or you can earn from platform ad-sharing programs. *Return horizon: Short-Term (potentially very fast, though not guaranteed).* A high-profile example is Addison Rae, who began posting while at LSU and rapidly gained a large following. Not everyone will blow up that fast, but even a few thousand engaged followers can bring in modest influencer income within a semester (e.g. free products or $50 for a post). The key is consistent content creation – one viral video can create immediate earning opportunities.

30. Selling Digital Products (E-books, Templates, Stock Photos): Create a product once and sell it repeatedly online. This could be an e-book (like a study guide, recipe book, or how-to manual), design templates (resumes, planners, etc.), or even a pack of stock photographs or music beats. Marketplaces like Gumroad, Etsy (for digital files), or Adobe Stock/Shutterstock (for photos) can list your items. *Return horizon: Short-Term.* After a few weeks of creation and posting, you can start seeing purchases. Notably, according to Canva photographer Diana Mironenko sells her travel photos as stock images and earns anywhere from $20 up to $700 per photo sold – a few popular images can generate significant passive income over months. Similarly, a student could sell a self-authored "Ultimate Calculus Cheat Sheet" PDF for $5 and steadily earn as new students buy it each semester, starting shortly after listing it online.

31. Subscription Box Service: Curate a monthly subscription box around a theme (snacks from around the world, self-care items, art supplies, etc.) and sell subscriptions to fellow students or online customers. While this requires planning and some upfront stocking, you can start small with a dozen subscribers and grow. For instance, a student might curate a "dorm survival box" with snacks, toiletries, and fun gadgets and charge a monthly fee. *Return horizon: Short-Term to Medium-Term.* It might take a couple of months to set up sourcing and marketing, but once launched, you get recurring income each subscription cycle. Within a few months, you could reach break-even and profitability. Each box shipped brings revenue that exceeds the cost if planned well, creating a steady stream of income. Subscription economics depend on fulfilment costs, churn, and shipping.

32. AI-Generated Digital Products: If you enjoy creating digital materials, you can use AI to produce high-quality templates, study guides, planners, flashcards, revision packs or other digital assets that can be sold repeatedly without extra work. AI helps you generate polished content quickly, refine explanations, design layouts and organize information into professional-looking products. You can list these items on marketplaces such as Etsy, Gumroad or student platforms that specialize in digital files.

Return horizon: Short-Term. Once your products are uploaded, you can start earning within weeks as students search for ready-made study aids before exams. For example, a student could use AI to create a complete revision pack for an economics module and sell it for $8 each – if 30 students buy it during exam season, that could be $240 earned from a single digital file. You get paid quickly, and the same product can keep selling long after it is created.

33. Developing Simple Apps or Websites for Passive Income: Invest a few weeks to build a simple mobile app or a content-based website that can generate ad revenue or micro-transactions. Think of an app like a basic to-do list, campus event tracker, or a fun game – something small but useful or entertaining. Publish it on app stores or host ads on the website. *Return horizon: Short-Term.* While a complex app can take longer, a basic one can be built in a matter of weeks and start earning modest revenue soon after launch via ads or a $0.99 app price. One student, for instance, created a "find a study spot" website for his college with ad banners; within a couple of months, local eateries were paying for ad spots, and he was seeing monthly ad income roll in during the semester. It won't be huge at first, but it's quick to start and can grow over time.

34. Event and Party Planning (Student Edition): Turn your knack for organization into a business by planning events – birthday parties, club socials, small conferences or game tournaments. Students often struggle to coordinate venues, music, and food on their own, so they might pay a peer to handle it. You can charge a flat fee or a percentage of the event budget. *Return horizon: Short-Term.* You might need a few weeks to plan an event, but you often get paid on the event date. If you plan a fraternity formal or a departmental workshop, you could negotiate a fee and get at least part of it upfront. After a couple successful events, word-of-mouth can land you more gigs within months. (One student event planner coordinated a professor's book launch reception on campus – she charged $300 for handling catering and logistics, finishing the job in a month and getting paid immediately after the event.)

35. Résumé and Cover Letter Writing Service: Many students and even recent grads need help polishing their résumés or application essays. If you have strong writing and formatting skills, offer a service to review and improve these documents for a fee. You can start by helping friends and then expand via referrals or online advertising to other campuses. Charge per document or offer bundle pricing for a full job application package. *Return horizon: Short-Term.* With some promotion, you could be getting clients within a few weeks. Each project might take a day or two and you get paid upon delivering the revised résumé or letter. By way of example, a student who was adept at career prep started advertising on LinkedIn and campus job boards – within a month, he had a queue of paying clients and was making a few hundred dollars each month helping peers land internships by refining their applications.

36. Online Language Teaching or Tutoring: If you are fluent in a second language (or even a programming language), you can teach it online to people around the world. Platforms like italki, Preply, or Chegg Tutors allow you to set up profile as a tutor. Alternatively, teach your native language to foreign students. This can be done over Zoom from your dorm room. *Return horizon: Short-Term.* Usually it takes a couple of weeks to get set up and find students, but then you'll have regular weekly sessions. Payment is often weekly or per session. For instance, an English-speaking student in Asia started tutoring conversational English to working professionals online; within a month she had a stable of regulars, tutoring evenings and earning a few hundred dollars a month which began essentially as soon as her first week of classes concluded (and payments came through).

37. Virtual Assistant Services: Work remotely as an assistant for entrepreneurs or small businesses. Tasks might include managing emails, scheduling appointments, doing research, or social media management. You can find such gigs on job boards or freelance sites – many busy professionals are open to hiring a part-time VA in a convenient time zone. You can do this on your own schedule from campus. *Return horizon: Short-Term.* You'll typically secure a client within a few weeks of pitching your services, and then you might be paid bi-weekly or monthly. It's a quick way to start earning a reliable income. (Imagine managing the inbox and calendar for an online coach – you spend an hour a day on it and invoice them monthly. You could start this in, say, October and by the end of the semester have a couple months of VA income in your bank account, all earned in your spare time.)

38. Creating and Selling NFTs or Digital Art: Tech-savvy or artistic students can dip into the digital art craze by creating NFTs (non-fungible tokens) – essentially digital collectibles or art pieces – and selling them on platforms like OpenSea. While the NFT market can be unpredictable, unique or meme-worthy creations have fetched significant sums even from young creators. *Return horizon: Short-Term (in terms of creating, though the payoff can be hit or miss).* You can design and mint an NFT collection in a matter of weeks. If it catches the internet's attention, sales can happen fast. A famous case: Sultan "Ghozali" Gustaf Al Ghozali, an Indonesian student, took daily selfie photos and listed them as NFTs – within a short time, his collection went viral and reached over $1 million in trading volume. While that level of success isn't typical, it shows how a digital art idea executed over a few weeks can suddenly yield significant wealth. Even on a smaller scale, selling a few pieces of digital art can bring a student hundreds of dollars relatively quickly.

39. Catering or Meal Prep Services: Start a small catering business for campus events or offer weekly meal prep to health-conscious or busy students. For example, you could cook and deliver healthy boxed lunches or dinners a few times a week on a subscription basis. If you enjoy cooking, this can turn into a profitable side venture. You might begin with club meetings or birthday parties to build reputation. *Return horizon: Short-Term.* Within a month or two of planning and word-of-mouth, you could have regular clients. You get paid per event or per week of meal service, which provides a steady cash flow. (One student team started a weekend barbecue catering service for tailgates – by mid-season they were catering an event almost every weekend, collecting payments each time and growing a nice bankroll over the semester.)

40. Thrifting & Upcycling Fashion: Thrift stores and garage sales are filled with potential treasures. If you have a sense of style, buy vintage or gently used clothing cheap, then upcycle or style them and resell for a profit. You can do this through an Instagram store, Depop, or at campus pop-up shops. For instance, add trendy embroidery to old denim jackets or convert sarees into fashionable scarves. Sustainable fashion is in demand, and you're essentially being paid to save clothes from landfill. *Return horizon: Short-Term.* Within a few weeks of sourcing and fixing up items, you can hold your first sale. Profits per piece might be moderate, but consistent flipping yields regular income. (A savvy student fashionista spent one month curating a rack of vintage '90s clothes from thrift stores and hosted a dorm boutique event – she sold out almost everything in one afternoon, doubling or tripling her money on each item. That upfront month of prep turned into a lump sum profit by event day.)

41. Opening an Etsy Shop for Handmade Goods: Take a creative hobby online by starting an Etsy store. Whether you make handmade jewelry, custom artwork, knitted items, or personalized gifts, Etsy gives you a global marketplace. Setting up a shop is straightforward. You'll need to produce some inventory or made-to-order listings, then you can start selling in weeks. *Return horizon: Short-Term.* It may take a few weeks to get your first sales as you build reviews and get found in Etsy search, but often a well-made unique item can start selling within the first month of listing. (For example, two college roommates began selling handmade campus-themed keychains on Etsy – within the first month they had dozens of orders from students and alumni, providing a nice side income relatively quickly.)

42. Freelance Video Editing: With the boom in online video content, many YouTubers, small businesses, or student organizations need help editing videos. If you're skilled with software like Adobe Premiere or Final Cut, offer editing services. This is something you can do on your own time, and deliver digitally. Clients will pay per video or per hour of editing. *Return horizon: Short-Term.* Once you land a couple of clients (which might take a couple of weeks of outreach), you could be consistently editing videos each week. You typically invoice after each project or on a weekly basis for quick payment. Demand is high – *"skilled video editors are in high demand with the rise of video content,"* as noted by industry reports. That means a competent student editor can fairly quickly start making a few hundred dollars a month editing wedding videos, promotional clips, or YouTube vlogs for others.

43. Music or Art Lessons: Monetize your talent in music or art by teaching others. For example, give beginner guitar or piano lessons, teach singing, or offer drawing and painting classes to kids or fellow students. You could do one-on-one lessons or small group workshops (even virtually via Zoom). Many parents look for affordable lessons from local college students for their children, and many peers might pay for a short course (like "learn guitar in 8 weeks"). *Return horizon: Short-Term.* Within a few weeks of advertising (through community boards or campus emails), you can get your first students and start the weekly lesson income. You're usually paid per lesson or per week. (One university violinist earned extra cash by teaching violin to two neighborhood middle schoolers, getting paid immediately at each lesson – after a semester, she not only made money but also built a resume for future music education roles.)

44. Starting a Podcast (and Monetizing It): Launch a podcast on a topic you're passionate or knowledgeable about – college life, sports analysis, true crime, study tips, anything. While it takes time to grow an audience, even in the short term you can benefit from small sponsorships (local businesses might sponsor a college-life podcast) or listener donations (via Patreon). You could also use the podcast to network or sell your own small products. *Return horizon: Short-Term (for initial income, Medium for significant income).* In a matter of months, you can produce a series of episodes and might attract a sponsor or two – perhaps your campus bookstore pays $50 for a mention, or a professor's startup sponsors you. It's modest at first but real money. For example, a trio of students started a finance podcast; by their tenth episode they had a local credit union sponsor them for $200 per month for a short ad slot – not huge money, but it basically paid for their equipment and some pizza, arriving just weeks after their podcast launch.

45. Launching a Custom Clothing Line: If you have fashion design aspirations, start on a small scale by creating custom clothing or streetwear. This could be tie-dye shirts, hand-painted sneakers, or apparel with your own designs printed in limited runs. Use social media to promote "drops" of your new creations. Initially you might sell to friends or via an Instagram Shop. *Return horizon: Short-Term to Medium-Term.* Designing and producing a batch might take a month or two, but once you drop them, you can make sales in a matter of days. Each drop puts money back in your pocket which you can reinvest in the next. (Consider the example of a college student who loves sneakers – he began customizing Nike Air Force 1s with unique artwork and sold them at a premium online. Within a couple of months, he had a waitlist of orders and was charging well for his time. The profits from his first few sales came quickly and funded more supplies to grow this mini business.) This can be risky only because it references a trademarked product in a business context. Not illegal, but you may want to make it generic.

46. Mobile App Development Services: Offer your coding skills to develop or improve mobile apps for others. There are many non-technical founders or small businesses that have app ideas but need a developer. As a student developer, you can undercut professional firm rates and still make good money. You might find gigs on freelance sites or even within your university (maybe a department wants an app). *Return horizon: Short-Term.* Landing a contract might take a few weeks of pitching, but once you do, you typically get paid in milestones or at project completion within a few months at most. Completing a small app for a client over a semester could net you a sizable sum. (E.g., a computer science student took on a project to build a simple scheduling app for a local gym – he charged $1,000, worked on it over about 8 weeks during evenings, and had the gym paying installments as each feature was finished, bringing in appreciable income before semester's end.)

47. AI-Powered Micro-Agencies: Students can now run one-person agencies offering services like social media management, video editing, branding, email marketing or ad optimization by using AI to handle much of the technical work. Instead of manually producing content, writing scripts or analyzing performance data, AI tools help you create polished posts, edit videos, draft campaigns and generate insights at professional quality and speed. You focus on client communication, strategy and final refinement while AI manages the heavy lifting. Start with local businesses around campus who need affordable, fast digital support, such as cafés, gyms or small online shops. You can offer monthly packages for content creation, lead generation or marketing optimization, and most businesses will happily pay for consistent output they cannot create themselves.

Return horizon: Short-Term. Within a few weeks of delivering results (such as improved engagement or better ad performance) you can secure ongoing retainers. Many students earn a few hundred dollars a month from only one or two clients, and with AI increasing your capacity, you can scale quickly without needing a team. Client retention depends on measurable results and clear expectations.

48. Interior Decorating or Organizing Services: If you have a flair for interior design or just enjoy organizing spaces, offer your eye for aesthetics to dorm-mates or local renters. For example, at the start of the school year, new students might pay for help to layout and decorate their dorm or apartment for comfort and style. Or busy individuals might pay someone to come organize their closet or kitchen. You can charge a flat fee for a one-day transformation. *Return horizon: Short-Term.* It might take you a couple of weeks to line up a client and plan, but each project itself is usually done in a day or two – and you get paid immediately upon completion. (One student turned her knack for Pinterest-worthy decor into a service: she advertised "dorm makeovers" for $100 plus cost of materials. She got a few clients at the beginning of the semester and earned a nice side income in under a month, with each makeover producing immediate payment as soon as the string lights were hung and the throw pillows arranged.)

49. Campus Equipment Rental Business: Invest in a few in-demand items that students need but may not own, and create a small rental pool. Examples: mini-fridges, microwaves, projectors, moving carts, or even bicycles. At the start of term or during special events, students could rent these from you instead of buying. You charge a rental fee (daily, weekly, or semester-long) and a security deposit. *Return horizon: Short-Term.* You'll spend some time acquiring items (perhaps even find used ones cheap) and advertising, but within the same semester you'll recoup costs. Let's say you buy 5 mini-fridges for $50 each over the summer – at move-in, you rent them out for $30/month each to international students or those in temporary housing. You'd earn back your investment in just over a month and make profit for each additional month. By finals, you collect your fridges to use again or resell. This model can produce solid cash within a single academic term.

50. Vending Machine or Snack Stand: With a bit of capital, place a vending machine (or even a simple snack cart) in a strategic location – perhaps with campus permission in a dorm lobby or local apartment building. Stock it with popular snacks or essentials (think ramen, energy drinks, chocolate, notebooks). Students will use it at odd hours when stores are closed. The markup provides your profit. *Return horizon: Short-Term.* After initial setup, you'll start seeing money come in daily from sales; you might break even on machine and stock costs in a few months, then it's steady profit. For example, a pair of business majors pooled funds to install a vending machine in an off-campus dorm building. They refilled it weekly and after a couple of months, it was generating **over** $500 in monthly revenue, much of which became profit once initial costs were paid off. It's a semi-passive hustle that can start paying out the same semester it's launched.

Medium-Term Business Ideas (Months to a Year, 51–75)

Medium-term business ideas require patience, planning, and steady commitment, but they open the door to far more substantial rewards. These are the ideas that typically take several months to a full year to come to life, because they involve building systems, developing products, testing markets, or attracting early customers. They demand more effort than quick or short-term ideas, yet they teach you how real businesses grow: through consistency, improvement, and iteration. The payoff is that, once established, these ventures can produce meaningful income, build valuable assets, and position you for long-term success far beyond your student years.

Table 30 highlights medium-term business ideas that require several months of steady effort but have the potential to become serious income streams once they mature. These ideas involve building real skills, creating assets, or developing systems that grow in value over time, making them ideal for students who want to move beyond short-term hustle and begin building ventures with lasting impact. This matters because medium-term ideas teach you how to create structure, improve products, and develop resilience, all of which are essential for long-term financial independence. Each of the ideas summarized in this table is explained in fuller detail in the sections that follow, giving you clear guidance on how to start, what you need, and how each option can work for you as a student.

No.	Title	Main Description	Is This Right for You?
	Table 30. SUMMARY OF MEDIUM-TERM BUSINESS IDEAS		
51	Launch a Tech Startup (Campus Beta)	Build a minimum viable product and test it on your university campus before expanding	Coding or product skills; patience; willingness to iterate
52	Small Food Business or Café Stand	Create a pop-up food outlet, late-night snack service, or small café concept for campus	Cooking skill; small equipment budget; consistency
53	Seasonal Franchise or Summer Business	Operate painting, cleaning, or landscaping franchises during holidays or peak seasons	Leadership; project coordination; ability to manage teams
54	Real Estate Wholesaling	Secure off-market property deals and assign contracts to investors for a fee	Negotiation; local property knowledge; no capital needed
55	Invent a Product & Crowdfund It	Build a prototype and raise funding on Kickstarter or Indiegogo	Creativity; basic prototyping; strong storytelling
56	Buy an Existing Small Business or Website	Acquire a small online business or micro-site and grow it	Due diligence; small capital; willingness to improve operations
57	Build a SaaS Tool	Create a software service that solves a recurring problem and charge recurring fees	Coding or technical collaboration; long-term improvement mindset
58	Grow a YouTube Channel	Produce content consistently until monetization unlocks and	Content focus; persistence; basic editing

No.	Title	Main Description	Is This Right for You?
		sponsor interest grows	
59	Build and Sell a Mobile App/Game	Develop a simple mobile app or game and sell it or monetize with ads	Coding skills; creative design; patient iteration
60	Launch Your Own Product Brand	Build a small product line (skincare, stationery, tech accessories) under one brand	Branding; basic supply chain setup; visual identity
61	Build a Blog or Niche Website	Create long-form content, grow traffic with SEO, monetize with ads and affiliates	Writing; research; consistency over months
62	Create an Online Course	Turn your expertise into recorded lessons for global learners	Subject knowledge; video capability; structured teaching
63	Build a Small Agency with Peers	Offer bundled services with a team (design, marketing, app dev, content)	Collaboration; project management; delivering high-quality work
64	College Admissions or Career Coaching	Help students with essays, applications, CVs, interview prep	Strong writing; credibility; ability to structure programs
65	Build an Online Community or Forum	Create a niche group and monetize premium access or sponsorships	Community engagement; consistent posting; clear niche
66	Sell Software Templates or Plugins	Develop templates, themes or plugin tools and sell on marketplaces	Coding; UI design; ability to improve tools over time
67	Launch a Niche Product Line	Build a brand around a specific idea (eco-products,	Creative branding; market research; small inventory budget

Table heading: **Table 30. SUMMARY OF MEDIUM-TERM BUSINESS IDEAS**

Table 30. SUMMARY OF MEDIUM-TERM BUSINESS IDEAS			
No.	Title	Main Description	Is This Right for You?
		campus gear, wellness kits)	
68	Urban Micro-Farming/Microgreens	Grow microgreens or herbs indoors and sell to restaurants or students	Small space; basic equipment; repeat harvesting cycles
69	Build a Campus Marketplace Platform	Create a student-only marketplace for buying, selling or swapping items	Simple coding; marketing to peers; moderation discipline
70	Grow a Large Instagram Theme Page	Build a high-follower niche page and monetize shout-outs or affiliate links	Content curation; consistency; understanding trends
71	Domain Name or Website Flipping	Buy undervalued domains or sites, improve them and resell at a profit	Eye for value; patience; small initial budget
72	Used Car Flipping	Buy older cars, repair lightly and resell at a profit	Mechanical skill; ability to inspect vehicles; modest capital
73	Recycling & Upcycling Business	Collect unwanted items, recycle or refurbish them and sell for profit	Logistics; storage space; environmental appeal
74	Seasonal Moving & Storage Service	Offer move-in, move-out and summer storage for students	Organization; transport access; peak-season commitment
75	Amazon FBA Private Label	Source products, brand them and sell via Amazon's fulfilment network	Product sourcing; small upfront capital; optimization skills

51. Launch a Tech Startup or App (Campus Beta): Have a startup idea? Use your time in school to build and launch it on a small scale, aiming for growth within a year. For example, develop a campus-focused app (like a marketplace or ride-sharing app for students) as your pilot. While this is more involved than freelancing, the payoff can be substantial if it gains traction. You might even join an accelerator or pitch in competitions for funding. *Return horizon: Medium-Term.* It typically takes a number of months to develop a minimum viable product and start gaining users/revenue. However, student startups can (reportedly) grow quickly once launched – Snapchat, for instance, was created in 2011 by Evan Spiegel and friends while they were undergraduates at Stanford, and within the first year it was exploding in popularity. Monetization (through ads or venture funding) followed soon after. You might not build the next Snapchat, but even a modest app with a few thousand users by year's end may attract paying advertisers or investors, setting you on a path to significant wealth.

52. Start a Small Food Business or Cafe Stand: If you're culinary-minded, consider opening a small-scale food outlet. This could be a late-night campus food cart (tacos, hot dogs, dumplings), a weekend farmer's market stall selling baked goods, or even a tiny pop-up café in a common area with university permission. You'll need to navigate food safety and perhaps permits, but it's doable and can be grown over time. *Return horizon: Medium-Term.* It may take a couple of months to plan, get equipment, and build a customer base. After that, consistent profits should roll in each week or month. One example: a student trio opened a weekend crêpe stall near campus; the first semester was slow, but by the second semester their stall was a campus fixture, netting them hundreds of dollars each weekend in profit. Within a year, they were so successful they contemplated opening a permanent café. The key is that a food business might not pay off in the first week, but give it a few months of tweaks and marketing, and it might become a reliable, even expanding, source of income.

53. Run a Seasonal Franchise or Summer Business: Many students use their summers to run franchise businesses like house painting, window cleaning, or landscaping under programs (ex:

131

College Pro Painters, Student Works). You operate in the summer and manage a team, then use the profits for school. It's hard work, but by the end of the season (a few months) you might make significant money and even continue part-time during the school year by managing crews remotely. *Return horizon: Medium-Term (a summer season).* You invest the early summer setting up, then realize profits toward summer's end. For instance, Cameron Herold ran a College Pro Painters franchise as a student – over three summers he earned about $60,000 in profit, paid his entire way through university, and even bought a house at 23. In his first summer he was already turning a profit after covering franchise fees and labor costs. This approach yields a lump sum that builds over a few months of effort each year.

54. Real Estate Wholesaling or House Flipping (Off-Campus): For the enterprising student in real estate, wholesaling involves finding great property deals (perhaps rundown houses near campus), getting them under contract, then assigning the contract to an investor for a fee – all without actually buying the property yourself. House flipping is more involved (buy, renovate, sell), but wholesaling can often be done with little or no capital. It can take a few months to close a deal, but the payout for a successful wholesale might be several thousand dollars. *Return horizon: Medium-Term (few months per deal).* You might spend 2–3 months networking, finding a distressed property, and lining up an investor buyer for it. Once the deal closes, you get an assignment fee immediately. Some ambitious students have pulled off deals like this: finding an off-campus house for cheap and connecting it with a developer and walking away with $5,000–$10,000 for a few weeks of legwork. It's not daily income, but one or two flips in a year might be a substantial financial boost.

55. Invent a Product and Crowdfund It: Have an idea for a physical product that solves a problem? Develop a prototype and launch a crowdfunding campaign on Kickstarter or Indiegogo. Many iconic products started as class projects or dorm-room inventions. By rallying support via crowdfunding, you get pre-orders (and funding) to manufacture the item. The entire cycle – from idea to funded production – might take the better part of a year, but the wealth potential is big. *Return horizon: Medium-Term.* Expect a few months of product development and campaign building, a month-long crowdfunding campaign, and then a few months to deliver the product. If successful, you essentially get paid (via backer pledges) up front. For example, a few engineering students designed a smart notebook and launched it on Kickstarter; in 60 days they raised $50,000. They used that money to produce the notebook and paid themselves a healthy founder's draw while still fulfilling orders. By the end of the campaign and production run (maybe 8–10 months total), they had a profitable mini-company. Even more famously, the founders of Snapchat first pitched their ephemeral messaging app as a class project in April 2011 and later built it into a product that took off globally while they were still students – not crowdfunded, but a reminder that campus innovations might turn into serious wealth within a year or two.

56. Buy an Existing Small Business or Website: Rather than starting from scratch, you can purchase a small cash-flowing business and grow it. This could be a local business (maybe a small cleaning route, a campus newspaper ad business, or a vending machine route) or an online business (like a content website or a dropshipping store someone wants to sell). Marketplaces like Flippa list small websites for sale, some under $1,000 that make steady monthly revenue. If you choose wisely and improve the operations, you might accelerate the earnings. *Return horizon: Medium-Term.* You'll invest some time in due diligence and transition, but within a couple of months you'll start receiving the ongoing income. Think of it like buying a rental property, but it's a business: you might buy a niche blog earning $100/month and through better SEO and content turn it into $300/month within a year – tripling income and also increasing the site's resale value for a future sale. Or buy a small landscaping client list from a graduating senior and service those clients yourself – you inherit immediate cash flow and could expand it over the season.

57. Build a Software as a Service (SaaS) Platform: If you can code (or partner with someone who does), consider developing a simple SaaS targeted at a niche need. It could be a tool for students (like a collaborative study app) or for small businesses (like a simple appointment scheduler). Charge users a monthly subscription. It will take time to build and gain users, but recurring revenue is powerful. *Return horizon: Medium-Term.* Perhaps you spend 4–6 months building an MVP and onboarding beta users (maybe offer a free trial period), and then conversion to paid users starts. By the end of the first year, you could have reliable monthly revenue. The growth might be slow and steady, but it compounds. (There's the story of Facebook starting in a Harvard dorm – it wasn't charging users, but it scaled tremendously within a year. On a smaller scale, say you create a SaaS for your college's club management or a note-taking organizer that 100 students pay $5/month for – that's $500/month revenue within a year of launching, and it can keep growing with each incoming class.)

58. Start a YouTube Channel (and grow it): While we mentioned content creation in short-term, building a significant YouTube channel often takes many months of consistent effort. With medium-term focus (6–12 months), you can produce a library of videos, grow subscribers, and unlock YouTube monetization (which requires 1,000 subscribers and 4,000 watch hours). Once you hit that, you earn ad revenue, and potentially sponsorship deals follow as your subscriber count climbs into the tens of thousands. *Return horizon: Medium-Term.* It might be 6 months before you see your first meaningful check, but by a year in, you could have a nice side income. Nate O'Brien, for instance, started a personal finance YouTube channel from his dorm in 2017; in the first couple of months he only got a handful of views, but he kept at it. Within two years, he had over 1.1 million subscribers and made $220,000 in 2019 from his channelthetilt.com. Not every case will be that explosive, but even a channel that grows to say 20k subscribers in a year can earn a few hundred dollars a month in ads and attract freebies or sponsorships – a solid reward for your consistency.

59. Develop and Sell a Mobile App or Game (Startup to Exit): If you create a mobile app or game that gains popularity, one medium-term play is to sell it outright to a larger company. This is essentially a mini "build-startup, then exit" strategy that can happen surprisingly quickly if your app is innovative. Tech companies scout for talent and products. *Return horizon: Medium-Term (a year or less to build value).* You spend some months developing the app and getting users; if it takes off even modestly, you might get acquisition offers. A legendary example: Nick D'Aloisio built an app called Summly at 15 and sold it to Yahoo for around $30 million when he was 17That was within roughly 18 months of launching the app – effectively turning a high school project into a multi-million dollar exit (and he became wealthy practically overnight when the deal closed). While that's an extreme, even a smaller app sale can net tens of thousands. Perhaps you create a useful study app, and an ed-tech company buys it from you for $20k-$50k – that's a life-changing sum to a student, earned by the end of the year after some intensive coding and marketing.

60. Create Your Own Product Line/Brand: Instead of just a single product, work over months to develop a cohesive brand with multiple products. For instance, a student entrepreneur might launch a small skincare line, a campus fashion brand, or a tech accessory line (like custom phone cases, laptop decals, etc.) with a unifying brand name and aesthetic. Over the course of a year, refine the products through feedback and expand the range. Sell online (your own site or marketplaces) and locally. The value here is that you're building brand equity – loyal customers who recognize the brand – which can lead to exponential growth and potentially attract investors or retailers. *Return horizon: Medium-Term.*

It might take close to a year to go from initial product to a modest but stable revenue stream and brand presence. But once established, a brand can really gain momentum. (Consider a student who starts making handmade organic soaps in their dorm – at first, it's just a soap or two sold at campus fairs. A year later, it's a named brand with a social media following, 10 different soap varieties, and a spot-on local store shelves. Now the monthly sales provide a reliable income, and the brand itself could be worth a lot. That brand-building effort over a year turned what was a hobby into a business with medium-term profits and long-term sale potential.)

61. Blogging and Niche Websites: Create a blog or content website targeting a specific niche (college productivity, vegan recipes on a budget, travel hacks for students, etc.) and consistently produce high-quality content. Use SEO techniques to grow organic traffic. Monetize through ads (Google AdSense or Mediavine, etc.), affiliate links, or sponsored posts. It's slow to start, but by the end of year one you might have a few thousand monthly readers which can bring in money. *Return horizon: Medium-Term.* Typically it takes 6+ months for a blog to gain traction on search engines and start earning more than pocket change, but steady growth follows. Michelle Schroeder-Gardner famously started her "Making Sense of Cents" personal finance blog while paying off student loans; within a year or so she discovered affiliate marketing and it turned into a money-making machine. Many student bloggers might earn a few hundred a month after a year of effort – not huge, but valuable semi-passive income that can scale. Plus, blogging builds a platform you can leverage for years (which becomes long-term wealth if you stick with it or even sell the site).

62. Develop an Online Course or Membership Community: Package your knowledge into a paid online course (video lessons, e-books, etc.) or create a membership site for exclusive content. Perhaps you've aced the GRE or a certain class – make a prep course for it. Or you're great at graphic design – create a "design for beginners" course. Platforms like Udemy or Teachable allow you to launch easily, or you can run a private Discord/Slack community with monthly dues where you share insights (e.g., an investing club or coding interview prep group). *Return horizon: Medium-Term.* You'll spend a few months building the course content and marketing it. Income might start as a trickle with your first few students but can ramp up with each cohort or as word spreads. By the time a year passes, you might have taught several batches of students. For example, a computer science student created a "Intro to Python for Absolute Beginners" course over one summer. By the next spring, he had run two sessions of it online with about 50 students each, charging $100 per student – that's $5,000 per session, effectively turning knowledge into a medium-term payday. The effort was upfront in creation; thereafter, each new group was mostly profit, showing how medium-term planning pays off.

63. Start a Small Agency with Peers: Team up with friends to create a mini-agency offering services like social media management, content creation, graphic design, or app development to clients. By combining skills, you can take on bigger projects than you could solo. Spend the first few months securing a couple of anchor clients (maybe a local business association, a startup, or your college's departments), then expand. Over a year, you can formalize processes and start to build a reputation beyond campus. *Return horizon: Medium-Term.* It might take 2–3 months to land and complete your first multi-faceted project as an agency, but as those wrap up and clients pay, you'll see larger chunks of income. By the end of the year, you could have a portfolio and several steady clients paying monthly retainers. (Imagine three friends – one coder, one designer, one marketer – form a digital agency. By spring, they land a contract to revamp a local restaurant's website, manage its Instagram, and do promotional videos for $1,500. They split the work and pay. Next, they target a bigger client, say a chain of cafes, and secure a $10k contract over summer. The agency's revenue grows project by project, and within a year they have a real business that could continue after graduation or be sold as a book of business.)

64. College Admissions or Career Consulting: Having successfully navigated college admissions or internship hunts yourself, you can counsel others. Medium-term, you can establish yourself as a go-to consultant for high schoolers aiming for college (helping with college essays, applications strategy) or for fellow students seeking top internships and jobs (resume review, interview coaching). This is a step up from the immediate individual resume service – you're packaging a more comprehensive advisory service. You might run multi-week coaching programs or workshops. *Return horizon: Medium-Term.* It takes time to build credibility and referrals in this space – perhaps a few months to get your first handful of clients and success stories – but by a year's time you could have a steady flow. Clients often pay in packages (which means larger sums). For instance, a student who got into an Ivy League could charge a high school student's family $1,000 for a few months of admissions coaching (with milestones for essays, applications, interview prep). After guiding several clients into good schools over a year, the demand and rates go up. Similarly, a senior who landed a top-tier consulting internship might run a summer bootcamp for underclassmen on recruitment, earning a sizable side income by program's end while also enhancing his own professional network.

65. Build an Online Community or Forum with Paid Features: Create a niche online forum or social community that gains a loyal user base, then introduce monetization in the form of premium memberships or sponsored content. For example, a student could start a forum for exchange students worldwide to share tips. Over months, as membership grows into the thousands, you could charge a small fee for access to exclusive sub-forums or events or get companies to sponsor and advertise to your community. *Return horizon: Medium-Term.* Community building is slower – expect to spend 6+ months to reach critical mass. But once you do, the revenue can start via subscriptions or partnerships. By the one-year mark, your community might be recognized in its niche. (Picture a scenario: You start a "Student Side Hustle Network" Facebook group or Discord in January. By June it has 5,000 members actively swapping advice. You then launch a $5/month "insider" tier for exclusive webinars and resources – even if only 200 join, that's $1,000/month recurring. You're monetizing a community you grew in under a year, and that income can increase as membership and engagement deepen.)

66. Sell Software Templates or Plugins: Develop digital products for other creators – for example, WordPress themes, website templates, Unity game assets, or app plugins – and sell them on marketplaces. Creating a high-quality template might take a month or two of coding/design, but once it's done, it can be sold repeatedly without much additional work. *Return horizon: Medium-Term.* It takes a bit to build and release the product and then for sales to ramp up as customers find it. However, by the second half of the year, you could be getting a steady trickle of sales. Some student developers have made respectable side income this way. (Case in point: a student developed a WordPress blog theme tailored for photographers and listed it on a marketplace. At first, just a few sales a month came in. But as he improved it and got reviews, it climbed the search. By year's end it was selling dozens of copies a month at $30 each, yielding a few hundred dollars per month in relatively passive income. The work was front-loaded in creating the template; the payoff continued as long as it sold.)

67. Launch a Niche Product Brand (Slow and Steady): Instead of a one-off product, nurture a brand in a specific niche over the course of a year. For example, create a line of eco-friendly school supplies (pens, notebooks) or a niche beauty product (like vegan lip balms) under your own brand name. Initially, you might sell at local markets or small retailers, then expand online. This approach is about gradually establishing brand identity and customer trust. *Return horizon: Medium-Term.* It's not an overnight cash-grab; profits might be reinvested at first. But within a year, you aim to break even and then see accelerating sales as word-of-mouth builds. A steady growth story: Two students started a sustainable fashion brand using upcycled materials. The first collection of 50 shirts took 3 months to make and sold slowly online. But each quarter, they released new designs, improved marketing on Instagram, and attended pop-ups. By the end of the year, their brand had a loyal following and monthly sales in the four figures, with healthy profit margins. The wealth is in both the immediate profit and the growing brand equity, which might be worth a lot if they continue (or even if they sell the brand down the line).

68. Urban Farming or Microgreen Business: If you have a green thumb, start a small urban farming venture. This could mean growing microgreens, mushrooms, or herbs in a spare room or campus greenhouse and selling them to local restaurants and farmers' markets. Alternatively, organize a community-supported agriculture (CSA) program where subscribers pay you to deliver fresh produce weekly (if you have access to some land or even a large rooftop). *Return horizon: Medium-Term.* You'll spend the first couple of months setting up and doing trial crops. Once the system is running, you can harvest and sell continuously. It typically takes a few growth cycles (weeks) to perfect yield and line up clients, but many microgreen businesses become profitable in under 6 months because microgreens grow in 1–2 weeks. (One student turned an old dorm basement into a microgreen farm under LED lights – he grew pea shoots, radish greens, etc. Every two weeks he harvested and sold trays to a few health-food cafes and directly to consumers at $20 per tray. After initial equipment costs, he was making a few hundred dollars a month by the second semester, with potential to expand by adding more trays or varieties each cycle.)

69. Campus Marketplace Platform: Create a platform (website or app) exclusively for students to buy, sell, or swap goods and services. Essentially, you become a middleman like a mini "Craigslist" or "Facebook Marketplace" just for your university or group of universities. You could monetize it through small transaction fees or local business ads. Building the platform and user base will take time, but once it's active, it can practically run itself with moderation. *Return horizon: Medium-Term.* It might take most of the academic year to get a significant portion of the student body using it. However, even before reaching critical mass, you could start earning via ads or premium features. (Imagine you launch a site called "Tiger Trade" for your college. In the fall, a few dozen posts appear – students selling used textbooks, offering tutoring, etc. By spring, you have thousands of users and local pizza shops paying to place banner ads for hungry deal-hunters. A comparable real concept was described where on smaller campuses a dedicated marketplace could thrive, monetized through advertising. By the end of the year, you might be collecting enough in ad revenue or sponsorship from the college (who appreciates the service) to call it a profitable venture, plus you could expand it to other campuses for even more growth.)

70. Instagram Theme Page with Monetization: Grow an Instagram page around a specific theme or niche (e.g. college memes, study tips aesthetic, dorm décor showcase, fitness motivation for students). Instead of focusing on personal influencing, theme pages aggregate content and attract followers interested in that theme. Over several months, you can accumulate a large following if the content resonates. Once you have, say, 50,000 followers, you can monetize by selling shoutouts (promos for other accounts or products), doing affiliate marketing, or even selling your own merchandise related to the theme. *Return horizon: Medium-Term.* Building a big audience takes months of consistent posting and engagement, but it's feasible within a year to reach meaningful size. For instance, a student created an Instagram page sharing funny relatable student life comics (curated and original). It took about 8 months to hit 60k followers. At that point, she started charging $30-$50 for 24-hour shoutouts to small brands or other pages, bringing in a couple hundred dollars per month with very little extra effort besides maintaining the page. As the page continued to grow beyond the first year, so did the income – a medium-term foundation for longer-term passive revenue or a valuable asset to sell.

71. Domain Name and Website Flipping: Acquire promising domain names or even whole starter websites, improve them, and sell for a profit. For domain names, you look for catchy, brandable, or keyword-rich .com domains (sometimes you can grab expired ones or think up new ones) and list them for sale. For websites, you might take a small content site with some traffic, polish the design or add content over a few months, then flip it on a marketplace for a higher price. *Return horizon: Medium-Term.* Holding domains might take months or years until the right buyer comes, but a portfolio of good domains could yield occasional big paydays. Website flipping can be done in 6–12 months turnaround. (Consider that someone bought the domain for a common phrase or future product – and then a company wants it. For example, if you had snapped up a domain like CampusRideShare.com cheaply and a startup comes along needing that, you could sell it for a few thousand. Or you buy a small blog making $10/month for $200, work on it to make $50/month through SEO improvements, then sell it for $1,500 (sites often sell for ~30× monthly revenue), effectively earning money from the monthly revenue and then a lump sum profit on sale, all within a year.)

72. Used Car Flipping: If you have mechanical savvy or know how to spot a deal, buy used cars at low prices, fix them up (or just clean and do minor touch-ups), and resell at a higher price. This can be done gradually – perhaps flip one car every month or two. Even a $500 profit per car can add up, and some flips might yield much more. You can start with very cheap cars and work up to nicer ones as your capital grows. *Return horizon: Medium-Term.* Each flip cycle might be a few weeks to a couple of months (finding the car, doing repairs, finding a buyer). Within a year, you might flip several vehicles. By the end of the year, not only have you pocketed profits, but you also have more cash to scale this side business or invest elsewhere. (There's a tale of a college student who started with $1,000 to buy an old Honda, fixed and resold it for $1,500, then repeated the process. After a year of occasional flips alongside classes, he had turned that $1,000 into $5,000+ and learned a ton about negotiation and auto mechanics. Each sale was a medium-term win – it didn't pay off daily, but every month or two he'd get a sizeable influx of cash.)

73. Recycling and Upcycling Service: Take the initiative in your community to collect and monetize recyclables or upcycle unwanted items into products. For example, gather scrap metal, old electronics, or bulk recyclables from campus move-out (lots of students throw away usable things in May). Sort and sell the raw materials to recycling centers or upcycle into something you can sell (turn old jeans into backpacks, or discarded wood pallets into furniture). It's both eco-friendly and potentially profitable. *Return horizon: Medium-Term.* It might take a few months to streamline collection and find buyers for materials or products. But you could see your first revenues as soon as you make your first bulk drop-off at a recycler or sale of an upcycled item, then scale up. One student project, at semester's end, they collected dozens of unwanted mini-fridges, lamps, and microwaves that students left behind. Over the summer they cleaned and stored them, then resold them to incoming students in the fall, making a few hundred dollars for a couple months of effort and storage – essentially being paid to recycle. Others have collected aluminum cans at campus events to redeem by the pound. Medium-term, you might establish agreements with dorms for regular collections and turn it into a recurring seasonal business that yields a reliable chunk of money each year.

74. Seasonal Moving/Storage Service: Every end-of-term, students need to move out, and at the start of term, move in. Offer a combined moving and summer storage service. For a fee, you pick up a student's boxes and furniture at move-out, store them over the summer in a rented locker or spare garage, and then deliver them back when school resumes. It's incredibly valuable for international or out-of-state students. Similarly, at graduation, offer affordable moving or shipping services for students transitioning elsewhere. *Return horizon: Medium-Term (seasonal cycle).* You'll mostly work and earn in these peak periods, which might not show profit until the cycle is complete (e.g., you collect money when returning items at the end of summer).

But within the span of that season or year, you'll see significant earnings concentrated in those months. (At one university, a pair of students did exactly this: they charged, say, $200 per dorm room for summer storage. They rented a storage unit and filled it with dozens of students' stuff in May, then returned everything in August. After expenses, they made a few thousand dollars each summer. Because of the timing, it's medium-term – planning starts a couple months ahead, and profit is realized at the end of summer when everything's delivered and payments are finalized. With each passing year, their client base grew, making this a reliable lucrative seasonal venture until they graduated, at which point they handed it off to younger students.)

75. Amazon FBA Private Label Business: Use Amazon's Fulfilled By Amazon (FBA) program to launch your own private label product. Essentially, you identify a simple product that's in demand, source it from a manufacturer (often overseas via Alibaba), maybe tweak or brand it with your own label, and send inventory to Amazon warehouses. Amazon handles storage, shipping, and even customer service, while you focus on product selection and marketing (improving the listing, getting reviews). For instance, you might sell a "college essentials kit" or a trendy study lamp under your brand. *Return horizon: Medium-Term.* The process of finding a product, getting samples, placing an order, and shipping to Amazon can take a few months. Once your product is live on Amazon, it might take another few weeks to gain visibility and sales momentum. But if you did your research right, by months 4–6 you could be selling steadily and profiting. For example, a student launched a private label stainless steel water bottle in a unique color targeting college athletes.

By the sixth month, he was selling a few hundred units a month with a ~$5 profit per unit after costs – translating to a nice side income. Over a year, he expanded to two more colors and saw his monthly profit grow correspondingly. The upfront work (and patience) of those initial months set up a nearly automated income stream (Amazon deposits your sales proceeds every two weeks) that can continue long-term or be sold as a business.

Long-Term Business Ideas (1+ Years Horizon, 76–100)

Long-term business ideas are the slow burners that create the deepest and most durable wealth. These projects often take a year or more to build because they involve developing real assets, establishing strong brands, acquiring property, building technology, or growing companies that can scale. They require vision, discipline, and the willingness to keep going long after the excitement has faded. But the reward is significant: long-term ideas compound, appreciate, and eventually generate income far beyond anything you could earn through short-term effort alone. These are the ventures that shape your financial future, create independence, and build foundations that can last a lifetime.

Table 31 presents long-term business and investment ideas that take years to build but create the deepest, most durable forms of wealth. These ideas require patience, discipline, and a willingness to think far beyond quick returns, making them ideal for students who want to anchor their financial future in assets, ownership, and compounding rather than short bursts of income. This matters because long-term ideas allow you to build systems, portfolios, and enterprises that grow in value long after the initial work is done, giving you security, independence, and the ability to make choices on your own terms. Each of the ideas summarized in this table is explained in fuller detail in the sections that follow, giving you clear guidance on how to start, what you need, and how each option can work for you as a student.

No.	Title	Main Description	Is This Right for You?
	Table 31.	**Summary of Long-Term Business Ideas**	
76	Found a Major Startup	Build a long-term, scalable company from a simple campus idea and refine it over time	Visionary mindset; persistence; product/tech skills; patience to grow steadily
77	House Hacking	Buy a small property, live in one part and rent out the rest to cover your mortgage	Basic property knowledge; small down payment; disciplined money management

No.	Title	Main Description	Is This Right for You?
	Table 31. SUMMARY OF LONG-TERM BUSINESS IDEAS		
78	Long-Term Index Fund Investing	Invest regularly in index funds and let compound interest build wealth over decades	Patience; consistency; minimal capital to start; suitable for all students
79	Dividend Investing	Build a portfolio of dividend-paying stocks for recurring income	Research skills; long-term view; reinvestment discipline
80	Long-Term Crypto Investing	Invest small amounts in major cryptocurrencies and hold for years	High risk tolerance; strong discipline; only invest what you can afford to lose
81	Strategic Use of Low-Interest Student Loans	Use low-interest student loans to free up cash for investment or entrepreneurship	Financial discipline; strict control; only appropriate for responsible students
82	Building a Personal Brand	Grow a multi-platform personal identity that monetizes through books, courses, sponsorships	Consistent content output; authenticity; persistence; niche clarity
83	Writing Books and Royalties	Write fiction or non-fiction and earn long-term royalties	Writing strength; creativity; patience; long sales tail
84	Scale a Small Business Into a Chain	Turn one successful campus business into multiple locations or franchises	Operational discipline; ability to replicate systems; leadership
85	Patenting an Invention	Create a unique product, secure a patent and license it for royalties	Inventive thinking; research; legal awareness; strong problem-solving
86	FIRE Strategy	Extreme saving and investing to reach early financial independence	High discipline; frugality; consistent investing; strong long-term planning
87	Build a Real Estate Portfolio	Own multiple rental properties accumulated gradually over 10–20 years	Understanding property; financing ability; patience; good maintenance planning
88	Build Exceptional Credit Early	Use credit responsibly to secure strong financial leverage later in life	Financial discipline; ability to avoid debt traps; organization
89	Retirement Accounts (Roth IRA etc.)	Invest early in retirement accounts to maximize long-term tax-free growth	Long-term thinking; consistency; basic investing knowledge

No.	Title	Main Description	Is This Right for You?
	Table 31. SUMMARY OF LONG-TERM BUSINESS IDEAS		
90	Build a Social or Green Enterprise	Launch a mission-driven company with long-term purpose and sustainable impact	Values-driven; patient; strong storytelling; partnership mindset
91	Extreme Frugality & Van Life Savings	Minimize living costs to redirect money into investments and long-term assets	Minimalist lifestyle; resilience; long-term savings goal
92	Aggressive Debt Payoff Then Invest	Pay down all debt early to free money for long-term investments	Discipline; consistency; budgeting skill
93	Leverage Student Discounts Into Investments	Save money with discounts and redirect the difference into long-term investments	Awareness; saving habit; long-term mindset
94	Build High-Income Skills	Invest years in mastering skills like coding, sales, design, writing or AI	Persistence; regular practice; professional ambition
95	Build a Diversified Wealth Portfolio	Spread investments across stocks, bonds, real estate and businesses	Patience; willingness to learn; steady investing
96	House Hacking 2.0 (Annual Property Stacking)	Buy one property every year or two, live in it, then convert it to a rental	Good credit; income stability; long-term planning
97	Entrepreneurship Through Equity	Prioritize roles or ventures where you own equity rather than simply earning salary	Risk tolerance; joining early-stage teams; big-picture vision
98	Invest in REITs and Real Assets	Earn long-term returns through real-estate-backed investment funds	Low capital requirement; desire for passive income; steady investor
99	Build a Local Multi-Business Portfolio	Own several complementary local businesses that reinforce each other	Operations mindset; strong community awareness; leadership
100	Continuous Reinvestment Strategy	Reinvest all profits to compound wealth across decades	Discipline; commitment; long-term vision; compounding mindset

76. Founding a Major Startup or Company: Take a big idea and run with it full throttle – this is the path of turning a dorm-room venture into a global company. It's the longest-term, highest-reward endeavor. You might spend over a year in development and user acquisition before seeing substantial profit, but the end goal is potentially massive wealth and impact. Think of the likes of Mark Zuckerberg, who created Facebook in his Harvard dorm room in 2004. It didn't make money right away, but fast forward: it reshaped the internet and made him one of the world's richest individuals. *Return horizon: Long-Term (1+ years).* In the early phase, any revenue often gets reinvested. You measure success in user growth or technology milestones, not immediate profit. With persistence, by year 2 or 3, you might have investors and significant market traction. Another example: the founders of Google were PhD students – their project took a few years to turn into a profitable company, but when it did, it became a trillion-dollar empire. Not every student startup becomes Facebook or Google, of course, but even a modest success can be life-changing. Founding a serious company is a long haul: expect late nights and maybe postponing earnings for a while. But if it succeeds, you build generational wealth. (Even on a smaller scale, say you start a tech company in college, raise some seed funding, and after 5 years sell the company for a few million – that is a long-term play that began in school and paid off later.)

77. House Hacking & Real Estate Investment: Use your time in college to start a real estate portfolio, which will appreciate and generate income over decades. "House hacking" is a popular strategy: buy a small multi-unit property (or a house with extra bedrooms) near campus, live in one part and rent out the others to cover the mortgage. As a student, you might do this with help from family or a FHA loan with low down payment. Over a year or two, the rental income pays your housing costs (and you learn landlord skills). Over longer periods, the property value often increases, building your equity. You can rinse and repeat by acquiring more properties after graduation. *Return horizon: Long-Term (appreciation / wealth over years).* In the short run, the benefit is reduced living expenses (immediate cashflow used to pay mortgage), but the real wealth comes when you sell or refinance properties years later. For instance, a Reddit user shared how they bought a house for $113,000 in college (2016) and sold it for $138,000 two years later in 2018, netting about $25k plus having lived nearly free. They then rolled that into bigger properties. This illustrates how a student can kickstart real estate wealth early. By the time you're in your late 20s, a house hack started at 21 could be a fully paid-off rental providing monthly income, or the equity could be used to invest further. Real estate is slow and steady but starting young means *time* does a lot of the work (compounding via property appreciation and mortgage paydown). It's a path to wealth that won't make you rich overnight but can make you a millionaire by mid-career if pursued diligently.

78. Long-Term Stock Market Investing (Index Funds): While not a "business" per se, investing consistently in the stock market is one of the most reliable ways to build wealth over the long term – and it's absolutely accessible to students. The idea is to start early (even with small amounts) and invest regularly in broad index funds or quality stocks, allowing compound interest to work magic over years. For example, you could put part of your side hustle earnings into an S&P 500 index fund each month. *Return horizon: Long-Term (5, 10, 20+ years)*. In the short run, markets can be volatile – you might even see a small loss in the first year or two. But historically, broad market indices have returned around 7–10% annually on average over decades. Starting at 20 instead of 30 can mean hundreds of thousands more by retirement due to compounding. A hypothetical: invest $100 a month starting at age 20 into an index fund earning ~8% a year. By age 65, that alone could grow to around $450,000 (and that's just with $100/month!). If you increase contributions as your income grows, you become a millionaire well before retirement. The key is consistency and patience. This idea doesn't give you flashy immediate returns – it's "get rich slowly." But it is practically guaranteed to build wealth if you stick with it. Many students ignore investing because the amounts seem small, but even $25 a week (perhaps what you save from a side gig or cutting costs) *invested* can turn into significant wealth over time. (As a concrete example, an early-20s investor on Reddit boasted about outperforming the market 3× since 2012, but even just matching the market would have grown his net worth tremendously by 2025. It's the long game – not exciting day trading, but steady growth that accelerates with time.)

79. Dividend Stock Investing for Passive Income: Another angle on stock investing is focusing on dividend-paying stocks or funds – essentially building a portfolio that generates regular cash payouts. Reinvest those dividends while you're young, and later, they can become a passive income stream. Over the long term, you can accumulate enough shares that the quarterly dividends are sizable enough to help pay bills or even allow early retirement. *Return horizon: Long-Term.* In the first year, you might see only a few dollars of dividends (e.g., $1000 invested at a 4% yield gives ~$40 a year). But if you keep adding and reinvesting, the snowball grows. After a decade of disciplined investing, it could be hundreds per month, and later thousands. Some young investors use a strategy of buying solid companies known for consistently raising their dividends (Dividend Aristocrats). They might not skyrocket in value overnight, but they provide increasing cash flow year after year. Picture by age 40, you own enough shares to receive $10,000 a year in dividends – that's like having a part-time job's income for doing nothing, and those dividends can still grow. There are true stories: a student starts investing small amounts in high-dividend index funds at 18, keeps at it through their 20s, and by their 30s they're covering a good chunk of their expenses purely from dividend checks. It's a wealth-building plan that emphasizes income generation, which can eventually free you from having to trade time for money.

80. Cryptocurrency and Long-Term Crypto Investing: Some students have made fortunes by getting into cryptocurrency early and holding on through volatility. This is a high-risk, potentially high-reward long-term play. If you believe in the technology, you might allocate a small portion of your money to major cryptocurrencies like Bitcoin or Ethereum (or carefully vetted projects) and plan to hold for many years, weathering the ups and downs. The idea is that in 5-10 years, these assets could be worth multiples of today's value if adoption continues. *Return horizon: Long-Term (and highly speculative).* You should only invest what you can afford to lose – crypto can swing wildly. But consider the example of Erik Finman, who at 12 years old in 2011 invested ~$1,000 in Bitcoin and other cryptos and by 18 became a self-made millionaire. He held on through big price fluctuations, and it paid off enormously. Another more recent case: many early-20s folks who bought into Ethereum or even certain altcoins in college around 2016–2017 saw life-changing gains by 2021 (some cashed out millions). Of course, many also lost or saw paper gains vanish if they didn't time it right. The long-term crypto strategy is essentially a belief in the future of decentralized finance or blockchain tech, coupled with patience. If it pans out, your tokens appreciated by, say, 10x or 100x over a decade. If not, you could lose most of it.

So, it's not a sure route to wealth, but it's one that has made real young millionaires (and also some cautionary tales). If you do go this route, diversifying and securing your assets (and maybe taking profits along the way) is wise. It's a bit like investing in internet startups in the '90s – huge potential but high uncertainty. Long-term minded crypto investors treat it like a 5+ year horizon gamble that could massively pay off or go to zero. Only pursue with eyes open and after research.

81. Using Student Loans as Investment Capital (Leverage): This is a controversial strategy but one that *has* been employed with dramatic success by a few – use the fact that student loans often have relatively low interest rates and invest the difference in something that yields higher returns. Essentially, if you have excess loan funds (after tuition/living expenses), rather than spending it, you invest it in assets (stocks, real estate, a business). The idea is that the returns outpace the loan interest, allowing you to pay back the loans and keep the profit. This requires discipline and is risky if investments underperform. *Return horizon: Long-Term.* You might only realize the true benefit after graduation when your investment has grown enough to cash out, cover the loan, and leave you with a profit. A *famous example* of a student leveraging loans is Dr. Ivan Misner (founder of BNI): he took a $5,000 student loan at low interest, used his own saved $5,000 as down payment on real estate instead of using it for tuition, and let the loan cover school. That real estate investment snowballed – he flipped properties repeatedly and eventually turned that initial $5k cash into a $1.8 million commercial property, all while repaying his student loan normally. He effectively arbitraged the low interest rate of the loan to get a high return in real estate. By the time the loan was due, he had well over enough assets to pay it. Again, this is not for the faint of heart or financially inexperienced – misuse of student loans can lead to debt trouble, and not every investment will succeed like Misner's.

But it demonstrates the principle of strategic leverage: using "other people's money" (in this case, federal loans) to invest long-term. If done responsibly (and likely with advice from financial mentors), it can accelerate wealth-building. Think of it like a low-interest business loan you happened to get because you're a student. Used wisely, by the time the loan's due, the investments could fund the payments and leave surplus wealth for you.

82. Building a Personal Brand/Media Empire: Take content creation to the highest level by establishing yourself as a cross-platform personal brand over several years – perhaps as a thought leader, entertainer, or expert – and then monetizing through multiple channels (books, speaking, courses, high-value sponsorships). Many famous entrepreneurs and influencers started in their college years or early 20s and over a decade turned into multimillion-dollar brands. This requires consistency, continuous skill improvement, and likely some pivoting as you find your true niche. *Return horizon: Long-Term.* In year 1 you might just have a modest blog or a small YouTube channel. In year 5, maybe a book deal or a TV appearance. By year 10, maybe your own media company. A great case study: Marques Brownlee (MKBHD) started making tech review videos as a high schooler and continued through college – by the time he graduated Stevens Institute in 2015, his YouTube tech channel was a "full-blown sensation" with a massive following. Now, a decade since he began, he's one of the top tech personalities on the internet, with his brand spanning merchandise, podcasts, etc., generating significant income. Another example: Tim Ferriss (author of *4-Hour Workweek*) built a personal brand in his 20s and now has books, a top podcast, equity deals – a whole ecosystem. The key is that you aren't just looking for ad revenue; you're positioning yourself as an authority or entertainer whose name alone carries weight, which opens *many* monetization avenues. It's a cumulative long game. But college is a great time to start – you have built-in network and content opportunities – and by consistently producing value and marketing yourself, you lay the groundwork for eventually very lucrative opportunities (for instance, being paid tens of thousands for speaking gigs, or launching a paid mastermind community, etc.). In short, slowly crafting a strong personal brand can eventually yield diverse income streams and opportunities that far exceed a normal job's pay, though it might take a decade to fully bloom.

83. Writing Books (and Earning Royalties for Years): Writing a book is often more about prestige than profit initially, but over the long term, a successful book (or series) can provide a steady trickle of royalty income and boost your career or brand to unlock more wealth. You could write non-fiction (perhaps based on an area of expertise or a personal journey) or fiction (maybe you have a novel in you). It might not pay much upfront – unless you get a nice advance – but if the book sells moderately well over time or becomes a cult classic, you literally earn money while you sleep through royalties. Furthermore, a book can lead to paid speaking, consulting, or a franchise (sequels, adaptations) which is where big money can come. *Return horizon: Long-Term.* The process of writing, editing, and publishing a book can easily take a year or more. You might see a small burst of royalties at launch, then a long tail of sales. For example, a student writes a guidebook "How to Graduate Debt-Free" based on interviews and research. It sells okay – maybe a few thousand copies over a couple of years. That could be a few thousand dollars in royalties coming in gradually. Not huge, but if they keep writing (new editions, related titles) this could stack. In fiction, consider authors like Christopher Paolini who wrote *Eragon* as a teen – by his early 20s it became a bestseller, spawning a series and a movie. He's set for life from something he started in high school. Even smaller scale: a self-published e-book on Amazon that consistently sells a few copies a day can earn a few hundred a month in royalties, year after year.

One creative strategy: use student loans (again) or free time to write the book now and let it pay you slowly over the long haul. You won't get rich quick, but two or three books earning modestly can be like a permanent side income. And if you strike gold with one, it can open the floodgates (future books get bigger advances, or you license film/TV rights, etc.). The main wealth-building is that you create an asset (intellectual property) that can pay off for many years – a very *long-term* approach indeed.

84. Expanding a Small Business into a Franchise or Chain: If you already started a small business in college (say a successful food cart, cleaning service, or tutoring company), think long-term about scaling it beyond yourself. This could mean opening a second and third location or franchising your model to other campuses. It could also mean staying involved as an owner but hiring managers to run daily operations while you focus on growth. Scaling a business typically takes years of refining processes and building capital, but that's how you turn a side hustle into an empire. *Return horizon: Long-Term.* In year 1 you perfect the model at one location, by year 3 you have three, by year 5 you're in multiple cities or have franchised to dozens of student-operators. The wealth comes not just from cumulative profits but from the increased *equity value* of a multi-unit business (which you could sell or continue to milk for cash flow). For instance, imagine you started a campus laundry service that did really well at your school. In a long-term play, you package the concept and franchise it to 50 other universities over a decade, collecting franchise fees and royalties from each. Or maybe you keep ownership and expand regionally, being the CEO. In 10 years, your small service could be a company with $5M revenue – which might be worth several times that if sold. There are real stories of students doing this: e.g., two college friends started a simple storage business (like the earlier storage idea) at their Ivy League – after graduation they raised funds and expanded to many campuses, eventually selling to a larger storage company for a hefty sum. Or Jeni Britton Bauer, who dropped out of college to start Jeni's Splendid Ice Creams; it started as one ice cream shop and over years grew into a nationwide premium ice cream brand (with dozens of scoop shops and pints in grocery stores), making her very wealthy. The lesson: if you have a proven small business, reinvest the earnings to scale it up systematically. It's a marathon, not a sprint – but the end result could be a chain or franchise bringing in seven figures, far beyond what a single location could do. This approach requires planning, leadership, and often financing, but it's how student side projects turn into real companies that build long-term wealth.

85. Patenting an Invention and Earning Royalties/Licensing: If you create a unique invention or piece of intellectual property during your studies (maybe through a senior project or research), securing a patent and licensing it to a company can yield long-term royalty income without you having to manufacture or market it yourself. Universities often have tech transfer offices for this reason. Alternatively, you might invent something independently and later strike a licensing deal. *Return horizon: Long-Term.* The patent process itself takes a couple of years and finding a licensee can also take time. But once licensed, you might get paid an upfront fee and ongoing royalties for 10-20 years (the life of a patent is typically 20 years). For example, suppose you design a new medical device or a software algorithm. A medical company or software firm might pay you, say, 5% of net sales that use your patented tech. If it becomes part of a blockbuster product, those royalties can be immense over time. Even smaller: a chemistry student patents a new biodegradable plastic formula; a packaging company licenses it and for each ton produced you get a small dollar amount – it doesn't seem like much, but over a decade as production scales, you might quietly earn tens of thousands or more.

One real anecdote: a group of students invented a better lithium battery anode and patented it; a big battery manufacturer licensed it and they receive milestone payments and a cut of every unit sold. They moved on to other pursuits, but that patent is like an annuity paying them for years. The key is the upfront work of invention and legal protection, then partnering with someone who can monetize it at scale. Many research students don't bother with patents, but if wealth is a goal, thinking like an inventor-entrepreneur can lead to a long-term passive income stream from something you create once. (Note: if invented as part of coursework or using university resources, check the intellectual property policies – sometimes the school claims partial ownership, but then you often share in royalties anyway.)

86. Financial Independence via Frugality and Investing (FIRE): Embrace a lifestyle strategy where you save and invest a very high percentage of your income from a young age with the aim to reach financial independence (where investment returns can cover your living expenses) well before traditional retirement age. This isn't a single "business" per se, but rather a long-term wealth-building plan that combines aggressive saving (often by *spending much less* than you earn, hence building wealth from what you don't spend) and wise investing. As a student, you start by keeping your cost of living low, avoiding unnecessary debt, and funneling any earnings (from jobs or side hustles) into investments (index funds, real estate, etc.). When you graduate and (hopefully) your income rises, you continue living like a student for a while and invest the difference. *Return horizon: Long-Term (10–20 years to freedom depending on savings rate).* This is basically the personal finance equivalent of a long-term business plan: you treat your personal finances like a company that needs to generate high profits (savings) which are then reinvested.

The eventual "exit" or payoff is that by your 30s or 40s, you have a nest egg that allows you to work on what you want (or not at all) without money worries. An example scenario: You live very frugally in your 20s, save 50%+ of your income, invest it primarily in index funds. If you manage to save, say, $25,000 a year for 15 years (and invest it), assuming ~7% growth, you'd have around $500k. If you scale up savings as your income grows, you could hit $1 million or more by your late 30s. At that point, you might choose to "retire" or semi-retire, living off the 4% rule (with $1M invested, 4% annual withdrawal = $40k/year, which is roughly what you might spend if you maintain a modest lifestyle). There are real young people doing this: some extreme cases like Mr. Money Mustache who retired at 30 by saving like crazy, or many anonymous FIRE bloggers who reached independence by 40. The wealth built here is not flashy Lamborghinis, but freedom – which is a form of wealth.

And ironically, once you're financially independent, you often have the flexibility to pursue entrepreneurial ideas or passion projects that can lead to even more wealth (because you're not tied to a paycheck). This strategy requires discipline and a long view – it's the tortoise, not the hare. But starting in college gives you a huge advantage: you learn to be happy living on less and investing more, which sets your "financial thermostat" at a level that makes early

155

independence achievable. By avoiding lifestyle inflation later and consistently investing, you essentially turn your life into a long-term wealth-generating enterprise, reaching a point where work becomes optional while your assets keep growing. (In summary, spend less, invest the rest might sound simple, but over 1–2 decades it's transformative, turning relatively ordinary incomes into substantial wealth.)

87. Real Estate Portfolio & Rental Income Empire: Think bigger than a single house hack – plan to accumulate multiple rental properties over the long term. Your college house hack (from idea #77) might just be the start. Reinvest the equity and cash flow into buying a second property after graduation, then a third, and so on. Perhaps diversify into different markets or property types (single-family homes, small multifamily, maybe eventually apartments or commercial properties). Over, say, 10–20 years, you could assemble a *portfolio* of properties that each generate rental income and appreciate in value.

Professional real estate investors often start small exactly like that one student house and then scale up through 1031 exchanges (tax-deferred trading up of properties) and smart use of leverage. *Return horizon: Long-Term (wealth snowballs with each property acquisition and market cycle).* In the short term, being a landlord can be a hassle and not very glamorous – you might be fixing toilets at 2am or dealing with vacancies. But the long-term effect is powerful: each property ideally pays for itself (tenants cover mortgage and expenses) and leaves a bit of profit. In 15–30 years, the mortgages are paid off, and suddenly you have tens of thousands in annual passive rental income, plus millions in property equity. For example, imagine by age 22 you have 1 rental (the house hack). By 30, you have 3 rentals (maybe you bought one every few years using savings and equity). By 40, perhaps 6 rentals (some small multifamily among them). If each nets $500 a month in today's dollars, that's $3,000/month or $36k/year passive income. Not enough to be rich, but it complements other investments. By the time you're 50 or 60, many of those mortgages could be paid off or rents much higher – maybe now it's $10k/month net. And along the way, you had the option to refinance or sell properties to tap into large sums (since real estate tends to rise in value long term). This kind of slow accumulation is how a lot of ordinary people become millionaires by retirement. Starting in your early 20s gives you a huge head start.

It's a get rich slow approach, but with much more certainty than trying to get rich quick. One specific illustration: That Reddit house hacker who made $25k profit selling one house reddit.com could have rolled that money into two more house down payments, rented them out, then a decade later maybe those houses double in value – he sells one, uses profit to pay off the other, now owns a house free and clear giving full rental income. That is how a single move in college can lead to an outright asset by your 30s. Multiply by repeating, and you have an empire. It requires patience, good credit, and willingness to manage properties or hire management. But as a long-term wealth plan, owning land and buildings tends to be a time-tested path – rent from others goes into your pocket, and the properties themselves often appreciate faster than inflation.

88. Building Credit and Financial Foundations Early: While not directly a "business," establishing an excellent credit score and financial habits as a student is an *investment* in your future ability to leverage opportunities. In the long run, a top-tier credit rating will save you tens of thousands in interest on mortgages or business loans, qualify you for higher credit limits (which can be used judiciously for investments or emergencies), and even open doors to rental properties or partnerships (many landlords and companies check credit). How to do this? Get a student credit card or secured card now, use it lightly and pay in full each month – by graduation, you have a solid credit history. Keep student debt low or paid down to improve your debt-to-credit ratio.

Essentially, you're treating your personal finances with the same seriousness as a business's finances. *Return horizon: Long-Term.* The benefits of a great credit score aren't immediately tangible like cash, but when, for example, you go to buy a house or need a business loan at 25 and you qualify for a 3.5% interest rate instead of 5.5% because of sterling credit, that can save you tens of thousands over the life of the loan – which is real wealth staying in your pocket instead of going to the bank. Or if a dream business opportunity arises and you need a quick line of credit, having built trust with banks means you can secure the funds cheaply. Think of credit-building as planting a fruit tree: takes time to grow, but once mature it bears fruit every season (in form of favorable financing). Many students neglect this and have to play catch-up later. By treating your credit score like an asset to be developed, you give your future self a powerful tool. For instance, Dr. Misner's story about leveraging a low-interest student loan worked partly because he had access to credit at a good rate – if he had terrible credit, he may not have gotten that loan or later mortgages.

Or consider a student who diligently uses a credit card and graduates with 750+ score – when they eventually start a business, a bank might lend them $50k working capital at a low rate, something a peer with bad credit couldn't get at all or would pay a premium for. Over a lifetime, the cumulative effect of lower interest and higher opportunities easily adds up to hundreds of thousands of dollars difference, essentially free money or money saved. So, investing time in understanding and building credit now is a long-term wealth move. Plus, it often correlates with generally good financial discipline (budgeting, avoiding high-interest debt), which means you're likely staying out of financial trouble and preserving wealth. In summary: make "you, Inc." financially healthy early – your "borrowing costs" will remain low and your ability to seize big investments (like real estate or big business ventures) on favorable terms stays high, translating into far greater net worth in the long run.

89. Early Retirement Accounts and Compound Interest (Roth IRA/401k): Start contributing to retirement accounts as soon as you have any income, even if it's a small part-time job during college. Take advantage of tax-advantaged accounts like a Roth IRA (in the US) while you're in a low tax bracket – money you put in grows tax-free and can be withdrawn tax-free in retirement. If you get a job with a 401k or similar, contribute enough to get the employer match (that's a 100% immediate return on that portion!). The magic here is compound interest over decades. The difference between starting at 22 vs. 32 can be enormous by age 60. *Return horizon: Long-Term.* This is about securing millionaire status by retirement at the latest, essentially guaranteeing long-term wealth if you follow through consistently. For example, if a 22-year-old grad invests $5,000 a year in a Roth IRA and gets, say, 8% average returns, by age 60 that single stream could be about $1.3 million. If they wait until 32 to start, at 60 it'd be maybe around half that. So those early contributions – even if small – are the most powerful dollars you'll ever invest (each has so much time to multiply).

A neat aspect of Roth IRAs: you pay taxes up front (when likely your income/tax rate is low as a student or new grad), and then never again – so all growth is completely tax-free. Imagine putting in $1,000 at age 20 into a growth stock fund; by age 70 that one contribution might be worth $16,000 (at 7% growth) – and all of it is yours, tax-free, if in a Roth. And you can withdraw contributions earlier if needed (though not gains) with no penalty – giving it some flexibility as a quasi-emergency fund. We often think of retirement savings as untouchable until old, but another angle: having a fat nest egg gives you flexibility to make career choices later that favor happiness over money, essentially "buying" you the freedom to switch to a passion job or start a business mid-career because you know your retirement is already well-funded. In sum, consistently investing in retirement accounts from a young age virtually secures long-term wealth on autopilot. It's the slow cooker approach: set it, forget it, and decades later feast on a substantial fortune. The key is to start early (in school or right after) and remain consistent. Those accounts benefit from professional management and sometimes employer contributions too, which accelerates growth. It's arguably the easiest wealth-building idea here – you just have to prioritize it and be patient.

90. Launch a "Green" or Social Enterprise and Grow It: Start a mission-driven business that tackles environmental or social issues, which can attract not only customers but also grants, impact investors, and loyal community support. Examples: a sustainable product line (like upcycled fashion which we mentioned in short-term, but think bigger scale), a company that hires marginalized populations, or a social venture like affordable education tech for underprivileged kids. These ventures often take time to build because you're balancing purpose and profit, but in the long run they can tap into additional resources (like government grants or partnerships with nonprofits) that purely commercial enterprises can't.

And the market for ethical and sustainable products is growing rapidly, meaning a small ethical brand can become a major player in a decade. *Return horizon: Long-Term.* You might scrape by or reinvest all earnings in the early years building credibility and refining your model. However, after some years, if successful, you not only have a profitable business but also one with a strong brand story that can charge premium prices or expand easily due to goodwill. For instance, Patagonia (the outdoor clothing brand) started as a niche climbing gear company with an eco-conscious ethos; over decades it became a billion-dollar enterprise beloved for its values. A student-scale example: say you start a zero-waste personal care products business (shampoo bars, reusable cotton swabs, etc.) and keep it going after college. The first couple of years, you maybe break even while building a customer base and figuring out supply chain. By year 5, you're in local stores and doing solid online sales, employing fellow alumni. By year 10, you might get acquired by a larger sustainable goods company or grow to nationwide distribution.

The wealth built isn't just in the steady profits, but the potential multiplier if you ever sell or merge (companies with authentic green missions can command high valuations due to brand loyalty). Additionally, social enterprises can open doors to alternative funding: you might win an innovation challenge, or get low-interest loans from impact funds, etc., which further propels growth. Essentially, playing the long game here means aligning with macro trends (like sustainability) and being patient as you carve out your piece of that future big market. It's deeply fulfilling to pursue as well, which can keep you motivated through the lean startup years until the venture thrives financially.

91. Extreme Frugality (Van Life or Minimalism) Leading to Investment Capital: We touched on van life in immediate savings (Idea #91 was living in a van to save $1,500/month), but let's frame it in a long-term wealth context. By choosing an ultra-low-cost lifestyle in your 20s (like living in a van, tiny home, or with many roommates, and keeping expenses minimal), you free up a huge portion of your income to invest. We discussed FIRE philosophy (Idea #86) generally; this is an extreme version suitable for the adventurous.

Rich Student. Poor Student.

A striking illustration of this logic appeared in a widely reported case from the United States. A University of Tennessee student converted a van into a basic living space in order to avoid paying rent while studying. By doing so, he reduced his housing and utility costs by approximately US$ 1,500 per month, equivalent to around US$ 18,000 per year. As reported at the time, this decision allowed him to redirect money that would otherwise have been spent on accommodation into savings and future investments, creating a substantial financial head start before graduation (Tabahriti, 2023).

The point is not that students should live in vans. The point is that cost structures are often more flexible than people assume. When expenses are deliberately reduced, even temporarily, the freed resources can be redeployed into assets, skills, or opportunities that compound over time.

The immediate effect is savings, but the ultimate effect is that you have a much larger investment portfolio much sooner. Many members of the FIRE community have done things like living in RVs, tiny homes, or house-sitting instead of renting to aggressively save and invest while young. The wealth built is not obvious day to day (because you're not spending, which sometimes feels like depriving yourself), but later, the compounding of those saved dollars invested makes you far wealthier than someone who had a typical expensive lifestyle. One could argue that money saved = money earned. If you save $10,000 by age 25 through extreme frugality and invest it, at 7% real growth, that's about $40,000 by age 45 and $80,000 by age 55 (without adding a penny). Multiply by several years of such saving and you see how some people manage to semi-retire by 40.

This approach is basically what Mr. Money Mustache did: he and his wife saved ~50–70% of their income by living simply (biking instead of owning cars, etc.) in their 20s and were able to retire by 30 on investment income. It's not about being cheap forever – it's about front-loading your investments so that later you can choose your lifestyle freely. So, while living in a van or a tiny dorm room with 3 roommates might not scream "wealth," it's *creating* wealth behind the scenes by allowing you to invest a lot early. This is a long-term play where the wealth payoff is the freedom to live however you want later, financed by the nest egg that your youthful discipline **built**.

92. Aggressively Paying Off Debt (and Then Investing):
High-interest debt is the inverse of an investment – paying it off is like
a guaranteed return (if you have a 15% interest credit card, paying it
off is like earning 15%). Many students graduate with loan debt. One
long-term strategy is to make debt elimination a top priority, even
above lifestyle or some investments, to free your future cash flow and
avoid tons of interest. For example, someone with $30k in student
loans at 6% could just pay minimums and take 10 years, spending over
$10k in interest. Or they could live frugally and pay it in 3 years, saving
most of that interest.

After that, the money that was going to loans each month can
now go into investments or business ventures. *Return horizon: Long-
Term.* Initially, your "return" is negative (you're just less negative by
killing debt). But within a few years, you shift to positive investing with
full force and no burdens. The wealth effect is clearer when you
consider opportunity cost: debt can hold you back from taking certain
risks or making certain investments. Once cleared, you can channel all
funds into growth. A concrete story: a pharmacist had $150k loans at
graduation. By living like a student on a resident's salary and side
hustling, she paid it off in 5 years instead of 20, saving tens of
thousands in interest.

After year 5, she took that hefty loan payment she'd been
making and redirected it into maxing out retirement accounts and
buying rental properties. By her late 30s, she ended up much wealthier
than peers who just made minimum payments (who were still paying
loans in their 30s). Destroying debt is an unsexy but crucial step to
building net worth – it's like climbing out of a hole before you can
stand tall. If you treat it as a part of your long-term plan (maybe even
refinancing to lower rates, paying principal early, etc.), you'll reach the
zero-debt mark sooner and then have more years for your money to
grow unencumbered. The long-term win is huge: thousands saved in
interest can instead generate thousands in returns for you. After all,
every dollar of debt paid off is an immediate increase in your net worth
(it's one less negative on the balance sheet), and once you're debt-free,
all future earnings can go towards asset building. Think of it as clearing
the runway so your wealth rocket can really take off without drag.

93. Leveraging Student Discounts and Programs to Invest the Difference: During your student years and even a bit beyond, you get a lot of perks – from discounted software and free banking to travel and entertainment deals. A savvy long-term wealth strategy is to *always* take advantage of these discounts and then consciously invest the money you didn't have to spend. For instance, your university might give you free access to premium software or research journals that a non-student might pay hundreds for – you can use that advantage if you start a side business (saving on software costs).

Or student discounts on public transport let you not need a car – you invest the thousands saved on car ownership. *Return horizon: Long-Term (small drip savings invested continuously).* No single discount makes you rich, but the practice of funneling all these small savings into investments over years can make a significant cumulative difference. For example, suppose being a student saves you $50/month on various subscriptions, $30 on transit, $20 on phone plan, etc., total maybe $100–$200/month. Instead of simply spending that elsewhere, you automatically transfer it to a brokerage account to buy index funds. Over a 4-year degree, even at $150/month average invested at 7%, you'd have around $8,000 by graduation just from exploiting discounts. Left invested until retirement, that could be tens of thousands. It's effectively *free money* doubling as seed investment capital. Another angle: use student loan cheap money (if you have it and it's low interest) to, say, buy a new laptop needed for your side hustle from the campus computer store at a student discount – that tool could earn you far more, and you got it cheaper and financed at low rate. Or there are programs like startup incubators for students that give grant money or free services – taking advantage positions you ahead with less outlay.

Long term, consistently thinking "how can I get this cheaper or free because I'm a student?" and then channeling the savings into wealth-building (instead of extra consumption) becomes a habit that serves you well beyond school. Even after graduating, many companies have "young professional" deals or you might still access alumni privileges – keep that frugal mindset as your income rises, and invest the margin. Over decades, those decisions might mean retiring years earlier or having a much larger estate. In summary, treat frugality not as deprivation but as profit maximization: every discount or deal increases your personal profit margin, which you invest for compound growth. It's a long-term mentality that your future self will greatly appreciate.

94. High-Income Skill Development (Investing in Yourself): One often overlooked wealth strategy is treating *skill acquisition* as a long-term investment that pays exponential dividends in earnings. This isn't a direct business idea, but it enables almost all other wealth pursuits to be more successful. If you deliberately spend your student years and early career years mastering high-value skills (coding, data science, public speaking, sales, digital marketing, bilingual fluency, etc.), you become capable of commanding higher salaries, consulting fees, or launching more profitable businesses down the road.

The return on investment for learning might not fully materialize for a few years, but once it does, it can continue for the rest of your life. *Return horizon: Long-Term.* You might grind for a couple of years practicing and learning with little extra income to show for it. Then suddenly you find that skill puts you in line for a promotion, or allows you to start a side consulting service at $100/hr. From that point onward, the financial payoff is continuous. For example, say you invest time to become a machine learning expert by 25 – maybe you earn an extra $20k/year because of that expertise. Over a 30-year career, that could be $600k+ extra (not even counting raises or equity that skill might also get you). Or you pour effort into improving as a communicator and leader – by your 30s you might be in executive roles or able to raise capital for a startup precisely because of those soft skills, translating to potentially millions in company value created.

Essentially, you (your knowledge and abilities) are the ultimate long-term asset. Unlike market investments, its value is more under your control. A student who recognizes this might, for instance, spend significant time outside class on coding projects, contributing to open source, etc., instead of partying – at 22 they might not have a dime more than their peers, but at 28 they could be a highly paid software engineer or running a thriving tech business, giving them a huge wealth trajectory. Or an entrepreneurial student might take public speaking and negotiation courses – by the time they're negotiating real estate deals or investor terms in their 30s, those skills could save or earn them hundreds of thousands better than an unskilled negotiator. It's hard to quantify exactly, but the richest individuals often point to specific skills or knowledge (technology, leadership, creative design, etc.) that were the cornerstone of their wealth-building. So in a concrete plan: allocate a portion of your time and maybe money each year to improving a skill that has market demand.

It could mean getting professional certifications, attending workshops, or doing self-driven projects that build a portfolio. The "compound interest" here is that better skills get you better opportunities which then further enhance your skills and network (a virtuous cycle). After a decade, the gap between someone who invested in themselves and someone who coasted is enormous. In short, long-term wealth often stems from personal growth – it's like planting a fruit tree that keeps giving fruit (income, business success) every year once mature. The earlier and more diligently you cultivate it (your skills), the bigger the harvest later on.

95. A Diversified Investment Portfolio and Passive Income Streams: As you progress, focus on **diversification** for stability and long-term growth. Build a portfolio that spans stocks, bonds, real estate, and perhaps ownership in businesses (your own or equity stakes in others' startups). Reinvest income to buy more assets. Over decades, this diversified approach protects you from major losses in any one area and leverages growth in multiple sectors. Eventually, you aim for multiple passive income streams: dividends from stocks, rental income, interest from bonds or peer-to-peer lending, royalties or business profit shares, etc. This way, your wealth isn't tied to any single source. *Return horizon: Long-Term (compounding and risk-managed growth over many years).* By age 40 or 50, someone who's been systematically diversifying and reinvesting since their 20s will have a significantly larger and more secure net worth than someone who chased one trend or stuck to one path. For example, imagine by 50 you have: a paid-off rental property yielding $15k/year, a stock portfolio yielding $10k/year in dividends, some bonds or REITs giving $5k/year, perhaps a small side business (maybe an online course or an app you built earlier) bringing $5k/year.

Individually, none of these alone might fully sustain you, but together that's $35k/year passive – which might cover a frugal lifestyle, and you can choose to work only if you want. Meanwhile, the underlying assets (property value, stock principal, business equity) are likely appreciating too. It's a slow accumulation, but quite feasible by methodically adding a bit to each category each year. Another angle: diversifying reduces volatility – you won't need to panic if the stock market crashes because your rentals and bonds still give income, etc., allowing you to stay the course and let things recover (which is key to long-term success).

Essentially, this is the endgame of many of the earlier ideas: turn short-term hustles into long-term holdings. You might use immediate and short-term ideas to earn money, medium-term ideas to grow it into serious capital, and then long-term, you park that capital in a broad range of income-producing assets. The result is lasting wealth that can withstand economic cycles and even be passed down generations. It's not flashy – you won't see huge overnight jumps, but steadily, year by year, your net worth and passive income snowball. Think of someone like Kevin O'Leary ("Mr. Wonderful" from Shark Tank) – he built a business (medium term), sold it big, then diversified into all sorts of investments generating passive income (long term). Now he often says, *"I get up in the morning, and money has come into my accounts from dozens of places – that's my definition of financial freedom."*

That's what a diversified portfolio aims for: many streams trickling in, collectively a river of financial security. To get there, plan early to allocate funds across different assets and keep learning about new investment opportunities (maybe adding a bit of crypto, or investing in a startup as an angel investor, etc., as you grow). By managing risk and not putting all eggs in one basket, you ensure you'll be wealthy in the long run *no matter which industries boom or bust*. This idea is essentially implementing the timeless advice: "Don't depend on one income. Make investments to create a second, third, and more streams of income." It's how long-term wealth is maintained.

96. House Hacking 2.0 – Real Estate "Stacking": Expand on the earlier house hacking concept by adopting a strategy known by some investors as the "stack" – each year or every couple of years, buy a new property (often using owner-occupied loans for low down payments), rent out your previous one, and move into the new one. In your 20s and 30s, you can do this multiple times. Each move, you acquire a new property with advantageous terms (since primary residence mortgages have lower rates), live there to fix it up and get favorable taxes, then add it to your rental portfolio when you move on.

Over, say, 10–15 years, you might accumulate 5+ properties this way. It's like serial house hacking: at any given time, you only have one set of housing expenses, but you keep turning past residences into income sources. *Return horizon: Long-Term (a decade or more to see the full effect)*. This requires willingness to move frequently and deal with being a landlord to multiple tenants, but the wealth build is substantial. For example, start at 22 with a duplex: live in one half, rent the other (cover mortgage). At 24, buy a bigger home with 3 bedrooms, rent out two to roommates – keep duplex fully rented now. At 27, buy another duplex or fourplex with an FHA loan (low down), move there, rent everything else. By 30, maybe a single-family home of your own as your "forever home" (or maybe you keep going with multi-units). At that point, you have maybe 3 or 4 properties producing cash flow and (if chosen in decent locations) likely appreciating. The tenants are effectively buying these houses for you over time (paying off mortgages). Come 40, perhaps two are paid off, the others well along, generating thousands a month net; come 50, all could be owned free and clear, generating a very solid passive income plus a large net worth in property equity. Not to mention you could leverage them sooner if needed (refi or sell one to fund something big).

This is a long game because it's not until you have several properties and significant principal paid down that you feel truly wealthy from it – early on, it's a lot of mortgages and maintenance. But as each loan gets paid off (or rents rise), your cash flow snowballs. A real-life parallel: I know of a teacher who did exactly this in her 20s-30s – by 50 she had a small apartment building, two duplexes, and a house, all paid off, providing more income than her teaching salary ever was, allowing her to retire early. It was a 25-year journey, but it made a middle-class paycheck stretch into multi-million net worth. So, House Hacking 2.0 is basically scaling up a property empire one comfortable step at a time – a very achievable approach for someone with patience and basic real estate savvy. It's the opposite of trying to flip houses for quick cash (risky); it's buy-and-hold, using favorable live-in financing, and letting tenants plus time do the heavy lifting. This is a concrete path to long-term wealth that many ordinary people have followed to become quite financially secure by middle age.

97. Entrepreneurship and Equity Building: Rather than seeking a high salary, focus on opportunities that give you equity (ownership) in a business, because equity can grow exponentially in value. This might mean *joining a startup early* (and getting stock options) or *founding/co-founding* your own and steadily increasing its value. It could even mean acquiring a small business and improving it (the "search fund" model some MBAs do).

The wealth here is usually realized in a long-term event, such as the sale of the company or through profit distributions once it matures. Equity is how many self-made millionaires in their 20s and 30s did it – not from salary, but from owning a piece of something that became much larger. *Return horizon: Long-Term (5-10+ years often for a significant exit).* For instance, you might slog for years at a startup for below-market pay, but then it IPOs or gets acquired and your tiny initial stake is suddenly worth $2 million. Or you grow your own company's revenue to $5M/year by your 40s, taking home far more than you would have as an employee, and you still own the asset (which you could maybe sell for another few million).

The risk is higher, and many startups fail, so this isn't a guaranteed path – but the strategy is to accumulate meaningful ownership shares in ventures with high upside. Even smaller scale: maybe you can negotiate a partnership in the local business you're helping to build (sweat equity). Over time, instead of just wages, you then get a slice of the pie as it grows. Mark Zuckerberg's dorm idea became a $100+ billion personal fortune because of equity (he owned ~25% of Facebook at IPO). A less extreme, say a startup engineer #5 at a company might get 0.5% equity; if that company becomes worth $500M in a decade, that's $2.5M stake – not bad for a decade of work (far beyond cumulative salary). The key is being strategic about where you work and what projects you devote your energy to: sometimes a lower immediate pay or more uncertainty is worth it for a chance at a large ownership outcome.

Networking, accelerators, and keeping an eye on emerging industries can help you find these opportunities. This is somewhat like venture capital applied to your career choices – you're investing your time and talent in exchange for equity. It may take multiple tries (perhaps you join two startups that go nowhere, but the third is a hit). Long-term, one success can outweigh the rest significantly.

Thus, if you have an appetite for entrepreneurship, focusing on equity positions from early on can lead to outsized long-term wealth. It's a contrast to a stable corporate career with steady raises – that might be safer but often caps out unless you climb to executive levels. The entrepreneurial equity route has a low floor but no ceiling. If you're willing to take that long-term bet on yourself (and maybe on some smart co-founders), it can be the quickest way to seven or eight figure net worth – bearing in mind that "quick" in equity terms often still means 7-10 years of grinding building that value before a liquidity event. As a student, you can start building things now or joining college-founded ventures to position yourself for this.

98. Investing in Real Estate Investment Trusts (REITs) and Real Assets: If being a landlord directly is not your thing, you can still invest in real estate and infrastructure long-term via vehicles like REITs (which trade like stocks but represent portfolios of properties) or funds that invest in toll roads, pipelines, cell towers, etc. These often yield higher dividends than stocks and appreciate over time.

Over decades, reinvesting those hefty dividends can significantly grow your wealth, and you never have to fix a toilet or deal with a tenant. It's a more hands-off way to diversify into real assets that tend to be inflation-resistant. *Return horizon: Long-Term.* You'll get slow and steady returns – perhaps a REIT yields 5% and grows modestly; with reinvestment, you might average 8-10% total returns. It's like a stock strategy but with usually more income component which you can reinvest or later use as passive cash flow. For example, if you start at 25 putting a couple thousand a year into REITs, by 55 that could be paying you the equivalent of a rental property's income stream, without you ever directly owning one. Some REITs own apartments, some own hospitals, some own data centers – you can pick segments you believe will thrive long term (like maybe data centers and cell towers for the 5G era).

These trust structures must pay out ~90% of income as dividends, so they are a nice long-term yield play. One could also invest in Farmland (through REITs or crowdfunding) which historically appreciates and generates rent – another inflation hedge. Or in broad commodities or gold as a small portion of a portfolio for diversification. The idea is by retirement or earlier, you have a chunk of money in these tangible asset-backed investments that keep churning out dividends or distributions, giving you financial stability even if, say, the tech stock market is volatile at the time.

It's long-term thinking in that you might not touch these investments for decades, but they quietly compound. Then later, they provide steady income (some retirees literally live off their REIT dividends and never touch principal). In sum, adding real assets to your long-term plan balances your wealth and often adds reliable income streams. It's about patience: you won't see dramatic growth year to year, but you'll wake up 20 years later with a very solid pile of assets that pay you regularly. As a student, maybe you start small with a $100 micro-investment in a REIT via an app and keep adding – it's sowing seeds that become an orchard of money trees eventually.

99. Urban Entrepreneurship and Compound Ventures: If you plan to stay in one city long-term, you can compound local business knowledge into wealth. For example, start with one business, master the market, then use the profits to open or acquire more in complementary fields. This is a bit like building a local conglomerate. Say you start a college moving service (from earlier ideas). Once it's stable, you notice a demand for storage, so you open a storage facility. Later, you spin off a packing supplies e-commerce store or a cleaning service. Each business feeds the others with referrals and customer base.

Over a long period, you become a bit of a local mogul with multiple income streams. *Return horizon: Long-Term.* It might take 5 years to get the first business self-sustaining, 10 to have a mini-empire of three interlocking businesses. But by year 15 or 20, you could step back and hire managers, enjoying semi-passive oversight of a whole portfolio of local ventures. Many family fortunes were built this way across generations – owning several key businesses in a region. For a student starting now, it could be as humble as doing campus deliveries on a bike; then by 40 owning a regional logistics company. The key is you reinvest locally, leverage reputation and knowledge of the community to expand horizontally (different ventures) or vertically (controlling supply chain).

Each new enterprise adds to your net worth and income, while also strengthening the others (for example, your cleaning business gets clients from your moving service's customer list, etc.). This requires significant long-term dedication and likely working smart with partnerships and possibly family involvement. But it's a path to *generational wealth*, as these businesses can be passed on or sold. The process is incremental – maybe every few years you launch or acquire one entity. A real example: someone starts with a single restaurant, uses profits to buy a food delivery operation, then a catering company, eventually owning a dozen restaurants... 30 years later they might be a multimillionaire from originally one eatery. Or a contractor who starts mowing lawns in college, then adds landscaping, then construction, then real estate development.

The synergy and compounding effect of understanding one field deeply and branching out can be huge. It's like planting one tree and then grafting branches to grow an orchard connected by roots. Locally focused, patiently grown ventures often lead to stable wealth that's resilient because it's diversified yet within your circle of competence. As an added bonus, you often become a community pillar (which brings networking advantages, possibly even political influence that can further protect and expand your wealth). This takes a *long* horizon view – you're not looking to cash out fast, you're building an empire brick by brick. But if you enjoy entrepreneurship, it's a fulfilling way to accrue assets and success over a lifetime and maybe leave a legacy.

100. Reinvesting and Compounding Everything (The Snowball Effect): Finally, perhaps the most important long-term strategy of all is continuous reinvestment – making your money work for you at every stage. This means when your side hustles profit, you don't blow it – you invest it in stocks, real estate, or back into a business. When those investments yield returns (interest, dividends, profits), you largely reinvest those as well. You allow the miracle of compounding to accelerate your wealth. By treating $1 earned as a seed to grow $10 over time, you create a snowball that becomes unstoppable.

This approach requires discipline and delayed gratification, but it is the core of most self-made wealthy individuals' stories. *Return horizon: Long-Term (compounding is slow at first, explosive later).* In practical terms, say at 22 you save $5,000. You invest in a mutual fund. By 30 it's maybe ~$10k. At 30, you add a $20k bonus from work; now $30k invested. By 40, that could be ~$60k if modest returns, plus you've added more along the way. At 40, you use $60k as down payment on a rental property while still contributing to investments. By 50, the property has appreciated and the stock portfolio grew – combined maybe $500k+. By 60, that could be $1M+.

The specifics will vary, but the principle is the same: don't interrupt the compounding by spending the golden eggs – let them hatch and create more eggs. You of course can and should enjoy life along the way but living below your means and consistently reinvesting spare income is the "secret" that isn't really a secret – it's just not as exciting as a get-rich-quick scheme, but it's far more reliable. Warren Buffett famously said the first rule of his wealth building was to not lose money – meaning he always sought steady growth and compounding without major setbacks. He also observed that wealth builds like a snowball rolling downhill – you have to give it enough runway (time) and pack it with more snow (reinvest) to see it really grow huge. So by making reinvestment a habit – whether it's financial investments, or plowing business profits back into expansion, or continually educating yourself (reinvesting in your human capital) – you set yourself up to benefit tremendously in the later years of the long term.

There's a point where your money makes more money in a year than you could in salary – that's when the snowball is essentially rolling under its own weight. For example, if by age 50 you've amassed $2M in various investments that yield an average of 5%, that's $100k/year growth without adding a dime – likely more than your annual contributions ever were. At that stage, you can choose to take foot off gas and let compounding continue or start harvesting some for your lifestyle or philanthropy. But getting there is all about those earlier choices to reinvest rather than indulge. One can still have fun and budget "play money," but the overarching mindset is that any money not immediately needed should be put to work earning more. Over 30-40 years, this mindset virtually guarantees substantial wealth, even if incomes were moderate. In essence, the long-term idea #100 encapsulates all previous 99: whatever path(s) you take to earn and save, keep feeding the wealth machine and let time and compound interest do their unparalleled magic. It's the ultimate wealth-building "strategy" – patience.

Peter J. Middlebrook

ABOUT THE AUTHOR

Peter J. Middlebrook is a self-made multi-millionaire, investor, entrepreneur and British economist whose real-world journey began far outside any classroom. Having left school with no formal qualifications, he hitchhiked from England to India in his early twenties, travelled up through Tibet into China when the Tibetan border first opened to foreigners, crossed by rail to Moscow on the Trans-Siberian, and later hitchhiked across the Sahara Desert before further trips to South America. These early journeys, combined with a voracious appetite for books from cultures across the world, shaped his understanding of global affairs, culture, economics and human resilience long before he entered university. He later earned a first-class honors degree in environmental studies from Northumbria University and a PhD from Durham University focused on Middle Eastern political economy.

Peter spent more than twenty-five years advising governments, multilateral organizations, corporations and entrepreneurs across over sixty countries. He has been an advisor to numerous Heads of State, supporting national development visions and large-scale reform agendas, and has drafted sustainable financing strategies for countries ranging from Indonesia and Malaysia to Botswana, Egypt and Bosnia, among others.

He is CEO of Geopolicity Inc., an international management and advisory firm headquartered in Dubai, and co-founder of Dignity

Rich Student. Poor Student.

Designed and Delivered Inc., a US-based company developing affordable shelter and housing solutions for homeless and displaced populations. A frequent keynote speaker at international summits and conferences, including the UN High-Level Political Forum, Peter's work has appeared on global media platforms such as BBC, CNN and Time Magazine. Beyond his professional work, he co-founded the Great Ethiopian Run, remains an active philanthropist, and is also a lifelong musician.

Rich Student. Poor Student draws directly from Peter's lived experience, from hitchhiking penniless across continents to building companies, advising world leaders and creating inter-generational wealth from a standing start. His journey reflects the central message of this book: that your future is shaped not by where you begin, but by how early you learn to think differently, seize opportunity and design a life built on clarity, discipline and abundance.

References

ABC News (2024). *HECS-HELP repayment changes and timelines.*

ABC News (Maguire & Rawling, 2024). *"The HECS threshold is being increased, and debts are being lowered but repayment times will take longer for some under a new proposal."* ABC News (Australia), 2 Nov 2024.

Barnes & Noble Education (2017). *"Barnes & Noble Education Acquires Student Brands."* Press release, 4 Aug 2017.

Best Colleges (2025). *"Average U.S. Student Loan Debt: 2025 Statistics."* Best Colleges Research [Online].

Brealey, R.A., Myers, S.C. and Allen, F. (2019). Principles of Corporate Finance. 13th edition. New York: McGraw-Hill Education.

CBS News / Associated Press (2017). *"Mark Zuckerberg returns to Harvard to deliver commencement speech."* CBS News, 25 May 2017.

Covey, S.R. (1989). The 7 Habits of Highly Effective People. New York: Free Press.

Dolan, B. (2025). *"Warren Buffett's Top Investing Rules: Timeless Advice for Success."* Investopedia, updated 16 Oct 2025.

Dolan, B. (2025). *Warren Buffett's top investing rules: Timeless advice for success.* Investopedia.

Eadicicco, L. (2017). *"WayUp Is a Booming Job-Hunting Site for Millennials."* TIME Magazine, 25 May 2017.

EdSurge (2019). *"Instructure Acquires Digital Portfolio Startup, Portfolium in $43 Million Deal."* EdSurge News, 24 Feb 2019.

Education Data Initiative (2025). *"Student Loan Debt Statistics."* Updated 8 Aug 2025.

Education Data Initiative (2025). *Student loan debt statistics.*

Ellsberg, M. (2011). The Education of Millionaires. Penguin. – Insights from self-made entrepreneurs on the real-world skills and mindset that traditional education often fails to provide.

Ferreira, R.C., Miranda, R.S. & Goldman, A. (2024). *"The Journey of CodeLab: How University Hackathons Built a Community of Engaged Students."* In *Proc. 8th Int'l Conf. on Game Jams, Hackathons and Game Creation Events*, Copenhagen, Oct 2024.

Ferriss, T. (2007). The 4-Hour Workweek. Crown Publishing. – Strategies for lifestyle design, productivity, and entrepreneurship, challenging conventional 9–5 career paths.

Finder (2025). *Average HECS-HELP debt in Australia.* Available at:
Gatto, J.T. (1992). Dumbing Us Down: The Hidden Curriculum of Compulsory Schooling. New Society. – A critique of the standard schooling system and its impact on students' individuality and creativity.

Government of Canada (2024). *Canada Student Financial Assistance Program Annual Report 2023–2024.* Employment and Social Development Canada.

Government of Canada (2024). *Canada student financial assistance program annual report 2023–2024.* Employment and Social Development Canada.

Grant, A. (2013). Give and Take. Viking. – Examination of how giving (helping others and contributing to society) can drive success and meaning in one's career and life.

Guillebeau, C. (2012). The $100 Startup. Crown Publishing. – Examples and guidance for launching micro-businesses with minimal capital, tailored for beginners and students.

Hopkins Consulting Agency (n.d.). *"Hopkins Consulting Agency."* Wikipedia [Online].

House of Commons Library (2025). *Student Loan Statistics.* Research Briefing by P. Bolton, Published 23 June 2025.

House of Commons Library (2025). *Student loan statistics*. Research Briefing by P. Bolton.

Illich, I. (1971). *Deschooling Society*. New York, NY: Harper & Row.

Kiyosaki, R.T. (2000). *Cashflow Quadrant: Rich Dad's Guide to Financial Freedom*. New York: Warner Business Books.

Kusimba, C.M. (2017). *The anthropology of money*. Annual Review of Anthropology, 46, pp. 379–397.

Ries, E. (2011). The Lean Startup. Crown Publishing. – Entrepreneurship framework emphasizing rapid iteration, validated learning, and agile business development.

Robin, V. & Dominguez, J. (1992). Your Money or Your Life. Viking. – A practical guide to financial literacy, transforming one's relationship with money and achieving financial freedom.

Robinson, K. & Aronica, L. (2015). Creative Schools. Viking. – A manifesto for transforming education, fostering creativity, personalized learning, and systemic change in schools.

Schroeder, A. (2008). *The Snowball: Warren Buffett and the Business of Life*. New York: Bantam Books.

Smithsonian Magazine (2019). *The history of money: From barter to banknotes*. Smithsonian Institution.

Stanley, T. & Danko, W. (1996). The Millionaire Next Door. Longstreet. – Research-based insights into the habits and lifestyles of self-made millionaires.

Tabahriti, S. (2023). *College student lives in a van to avoid rent and save thousands of dollars a year*. Business Insider.

Thiel, P. & Masters, B. (2014). Zero to One. Crown Publishing. – Notes on startups and building the future, focusing on creating innovative, value-driven enterprises from scratch.

Rich Student. Poor Student.

U.S. Bureau of Labor Statistics (2025). *"Usual Weekly Earnings of Wage and Salary Workers, Second Quarter 2025."* U.S. Dept. of Labor News Release, 22 July 2025.

Unibuddy (2025). *"About Our Company."* Unibuddy.com [Online].
Whitten, R. (2025). *"Student HECS-HELP debt statistics."* Finder (Australia), updated 27 Mar 2025.

Wikipedia (2023). *"Michael Nixon."* Wikimedia Foundation.

Wikipedia (2023). *"Uniplaces."* Wikimedia Foundation

Yunus, M. (2007). Creating a World Without Poverty. PublicAffairs. – Pioneering vision of social business and how students and entrepreneurs can combine innovation with social impact for the greater good

www.ingramcontent.com/pod-product-compliance
Lightning Source LLC
Chambersburg PA
CBHW071551200326
41519CB00021BB/6696